HKAC

MAR   2016

"God created this diversity among human beings in race, color, and ethnicity to test us in doing good deeds. Islam teaches us that there is no compulsion in faith; all humans are free to practice their religion. These golden principles are the guidelines for Muslims in dealing with non-Muslims to live in peace with their non-Muslim neighbors. We live as part of a worldwide human community that is at war with itself. Unfortunately, these conflicts are both justified and emotionally intensified by religions. After all, the Qur'an preaches that all men are created equal. For this reason, I wholeheartedly endorse Josh's *How Not to Kill a Muslim* project!"

—Amir Arain,
Vanderbilt University/Islamic Center of Nashville, Nashville, TN

"Josh Graves undertakes a critical issue of our times and does so with empathy, sensitivity, and accuracy. *How Not to Kill a Muslim* is more than a mere corrective in the challenges of interfaith understanding. It combines personal account with research data, history, and theology into a readable narrative that will be of benefit not only to Christians and Muslims, but also to all who are interested in the mission of humanity."

—Saeed A. Kahn, Professor of Religious Studies,
Wayne State University, Detroit, MI

"In my role as chaplain on a college campus, I often interact with young Christians who are eager to love their Muslim neighbors in a Christlike way, but don't know how or where to start. Josh Graves has done them, and all of us who care about such relationships, a great favor. Here is a book that testifies to the generous way of Christ in a multifaith world, and invites Christians into the high calling of Jesus's greatest commandment."

—Craig Kocher, University Chaplain,
Richmond University, Richmond, VA

"This book wasn't born from conversations with a literary creative team as they threw ideas on a white board. It came to life because Josh Graves dangerously walks the streets of America asking pressing questions about the challenges we face and how Jesus' words and life speak into those challenges. The conversation quickly shifts in the Christian-Muslim dialogue when the primary lens is that humanity has been created in the image of God. As a Jesus-follower, pastor, prophet, and author, Josh Graves urges us to engage the dialogue with a new lens—a new way of seeing. The future health of our world may just depend on it."

—Josh Ross, Lead Minister,
Sycamore View Church, Memphis, TN, and author of *Scarred Faith*

"I would never read or recommend this book if I didn't know Muslim men and women. Growing up in a small country church, Islam wasn't something that we talked about a lot. However, my wife grew up with a Muslim stepfather, and once I met him I knew that the old stereotypes wouldn't work anymore. Since then, I've had hundreds of conversations with sincere, devout Muslim men and women who believe in the God of Abraham and are fascinated with Jesus. Josh has written a great resource for what it looks like to have theological conversations with people that we disagree with (and have more in common with than we thought). In the book of Acts, Paul is accused of disturbing the peace by naming Jesus as King. The people start a Riot and are about to murder some Christians. And then one of the more levelheaded people calms the mob down with a brilliant insight. He says, 'You have brought these men here, though they have neither robbed temples nor blasphemed our goddess.' Paul, the first missionary, somehow waded through the waters of first-century pluralism, telling people that Jesus was Lord, without blaspheming their gods. For anyone interested in thinking like the first Christians did, this book is a great resource for understanding our neighbors and opening up dialogue."

—Jonathan Storment, Lead Minister,
Highland Church, Abilene, TX, and author of *How to Start a Riot*

How *Not* to
Kill a Muslim

How **NOT** to Kill a Muslim

A Manifesto of Hope for Christianity and Islam in North America

Joshua Graves

 CASCADE *Books* · Eugene, Oregon

HOW *NOT* TO KILL A MUSLIM
A Manifesto of Hope for Christianity and Islam in North America

Cascade Books
An Imprint of Wipf and Stock Publishers
199 W. 8th Ave., Suite 3
Eugene, OR 97401

www.wipfandstock.com

ISBN 13: 978-1-62564-858-7

Cataloguing-in-Publication Data

Graves, Joshua, 1979–

How *not* to kill a Muslim : a manifesto of hope for Christianity and Islam in North America / Joshua Graves.

xvi + 130 p. ; 23 cm. Includes bibliographical references.

ISBN 13: 978-1-62564-858-7

1. Islam—United States. 2. Christianity—United States. 3. Islam—Relations—Christianity. 4. Christianity and other religions—Islam. I. Title.

BP67.U6 G73 2015

Manufactured in the U.S.A.   04/10/2015

For my parents, Phil and Kathy Graves:
You taught me how to *see*

Contents

Preface

THE FOLLOWING 208 WORDS let you know exactly what you are getting into.

The relationship between American Muslims and Christians is arguably one of the most pressing issues of our time. How might Christians learn to love and see American Muslims as our neighbors? What practices and attitudes might emerge from such an exploration?

How Not *to Kill a Muslim* is primarily focused on the relationship and responsibility of Christians toward Muslims within the context of North America. It explores the cultural and religious biases embedded within Protestant evangelical Christianity and demonstrates strategies for dialogue, appreciation, understanding, and shared life between Christians and Muslims living in the United States.

Using a combination of narrative biblical interpretation, contemporary cultural analysis, a survey of socioeconomic stereotypes, and the Participatory Action Research (PAR) method, this project demonstrates that the problematic attitudes, beliefs, and actions of (evangelical) Christians toward American Muslims can be significantly altered through creative and intentional scriptural teaching (Luke 10:25–37), conversation, study, pop-culture analysis, and reflection. The primary target audience for this project: ministers, progressive leaders, and cultural agents of spiritual subversion.

The entire work is based upon Jesus' insistence—multiple times in the Gospel accounts of the Christian New Testament—that the greatest duty of all humans is to love God and to love others.

I have found this to be the most difficult and elusive pursuit of my life. Yet, for me, it's the only life worth living.

Acknowledgments

I AM INDEBTED TO many sisters and brothers in the faith. David Bartlett, Mark Douglas, Barbara Brown Taylor, Walter Brueggemann, and Chuck Campbell (current and former professors at Columbia Theological Seminary, or CTS) helped me shape this project as I completed a doctorate from 2008 to 2012. A good amount of this material is built upon the reading, preparation, classes, lectures, papers, conversations, and work I did to earn the degree. I found CTS to be a place where big questions are not only permitted, they are expected. It was a great honor to sit at the feet of these rabbis.

Dr. Amy-Jill Levine, one of the finest New Testament scholars in the world (Vanderbilt Divinity School), for her writing, conversation, challenge, and encouragement over the last several years. Judaism and Christianity in America are better thanks to your work, Dr. Levine.

Otter Creek Church of Christ (www.ottercreek.org)—especially the shepherds and ministry team—for being the kind of community that dreams big about the kingdom of God.

Lee Camp for the having the guts to live, teach, and write about Jesus' kingdom in provocative ways. His influence on me in the past (Lipscomb University's Hazelip School of Theology, where I earned an MDiv) and in the present (*Who Is My Enemy?*, published by Brazos) continues to challenge my vision. It's an honor to be part of the same community of faith with you and Laura.

Imam Mohamed Ahmed and Dr. Amir Arain, important Islamic leaders in Nashville, for friendship and careful critique. They lead the Islamic Center of Nashville with grace and dignity.

The Ferdowsi family of Nashville for providing space to test this material among Christians, Jews, Baha'is, and Muslims. Especially Aram Ferdowsi and Kimia Kline.

Father Charlie Strobel for modeling radical table hospitality in Nashville for almost four decades. Every pastor needs a priest; Strobel has been that for me.

Jason Graves, Randy Harris, Josh Ross, Chris Seidman, Mike Cope, Sara Barton, Rhonda Lowry, John York, Rubel Shelly, Rick Atchley, John Barton, Wade Hodges, Luke Norsworthy, Jonathan Storment, Patrick Mead, and Ian Cron for refining my sloppy thinking and bolstering my faith on such weighty matters. Quick to disagree and quick to forgive. The best of partners.

Brad Crisler, David Rubio, Mike Runcie, Patrick Chappell, Jackie Halstead, Ken Switzer, Randal Wilcher, and George Goldman, for great conversations about the nature of faith in the twenty-first century.

My parents, Phil and Kathy Graves, for first teaching me *how to see people*. The greatest gift a parent can give to their child is the ability to see.

Most importantly . . . Kara, Lucas, and Finn for allowing my early morning and late evening study/writing on a subject that caused and *still causes* a fire to rise up in my belly. Kara—your humor, wit, insight, and stories always sustain me. I hope the world you live in is slightly better because of my work. You are the three most important relationships in my life. We are building something beautiful together.

Introduction

That Fire in My Belly

> The church doesn't need to provide nineteenth-century answers to sixteenth-century questions. The church should offer twenty-first-century answers to first-century questions.
>
> —N. T. Wright

I'VE WRITTEN TWO BOOKS prior to this one (*The Feast* in 2009, and, with Chris Seidman, *Heaven on Earth* in 2012). But this book—*How Not to Kill a Muslim*—is writing me. I have to write this book. Sometimes we grab hold of truth. Sometimes truth grabs hold of us. This is a witness to the latter not the former.

Like an internal ethical exorcism, I cannot keep the contents inside.

This book's been in me for some time, and I am going to get it out. I was raised twenty minutes from the largest Arab population in the world outside of the Middle East. While the suburban East Detroit neighborhood I grew up in was a world away from Muslims and Christians living in Dearborn, I was aware that there were *others*—there was "us" and there was "them"—black and white, Protestant and Catholic, Muslim and Christian.

I now live in Nashville—almost six hundred miles from where I grew up. Yet the tension that has existed in Detroit is a tension now being felt all over the United States—from Murfreesboro, Tennessee, to Los Angeles, from Atlanta to Manhattan. The tension between Muslims and Christians in the United States is not going to magically disappear. It is real. And it is an opportunity for remarkable progress.

Today, Christians and Muslims make up half the world's population.[1] Let that sink in. Of the seven billion people inhabiting the earth, half look to Jesus or to the Qur'an for religious, political, and emotional guidance. We have to learn how to live together, and how to do it *well*. Living together is not the same as existing together, not the same as tolerating each other. If the problem of the nineteenth and twentieth centuries was the color line (black and white), the problem of the twenty-first century is the conflict arising in places where crescent and cross collide.

The tragedy of September 11, 2001, continues to shape American Christians' perceptions of American Muslims in negative and toxic fashion. It is time for American Christians to do our homework—to move beyond shallow stereotypes and to realize that Islam is a large, diverse religious movement.

Is there anyone else out there who feels the same?

I want to help shrink the one-hundred-year rule. Let me explain.

Some observers of Western culture believe it will take Jews one hundred years to forgive and reconcile with Germany (and other European countries) for the loss of six million Jewish brothers and sisters. Some likewise believe it will take Rwandans (Hutus and Tutsis) one hundred years to truly trust each other. The same is true of blacks and whites in South Africa.

One hundred years elapsed between the end of the Civil War and the passage of the Civil Rights Act of 1964 and the Voting Rights Act of 1965.

It took one hundred years for Protestant reformers to fully embrace the witness of Anabaptists—radicals who took the Sermon on the Mount seriously. One hundred years for the reformers to stop killing Anabaptists.

Jews and the Third Reich, Hutus and Tutsis, blacks and whites, Protestants and Anabaptists.

Now, both internationally and right here on American soil, we see the "us versus them" saga being played out in the conflicts between Christians and Muslims. Although different from the previous examples, tension and animosity run rampant on both sides.

Same song, different verse. Suspicion, distrust, anger.

Time moves too slowly. We don't have another one hundred years before Christians and Muslims can live, work, and share life together in these United States. I want to be a part of a movement that is committed

1. I will bring your attention to this fact again and again in the chapters that follow.

to shrinking the one-hundred-year rule. Because I'm a Christian, I write this subjectively from one Christian perspective. I do not write with a voice of authority or power but as a simple local church pastor trying to see the things of heaven come true in the realm of earth.

The future belongs to those who *see* as Jesus sees. Forty thousand words coming at you. There it is. Literally and metaphorically.

Grace and Peace,

Josh Graves
Easter Sunday 2014

1

We Are the Stories
We Tell Ourselves

N. Scott Momaday, American Indian writer and retired professor of literature at the University of Southern California, offers a critical *wisdom story* for the beginning of our journey together. When Momaday was a young boy, his father woke him early in the morning and said, "I want you to get up and go with me." His father took him by the hand and led him, sleepy, to the house of an old squaw (his words), and left him, saying, "I'll get you this afternoon." All day long the old squaw of the Kiowa tribe told stories to the boy, sang songs, described rituals, and told the history of the Kiowa. She told the boy how the tribe began out of a hollow log in the Yellowstone River, of the migration southward, the wars with other tribes, the great blizzards, the buffalo hunt, the coming of the white man, starvation, the diminished tribe, and, finally, being moved to a reservation, confinement. At sunset his father came and said, "Son, it's time to go."

Momaday—as a much older man—later reflected, "I left her house a Kiowa."[1]

To be Christian (or Jewish, Muslim, Baha'i, or Buddhist) is to be enrolled in a particular story, and anybody who can't remember any further

---

1. Quoted in Craddock, *Collected Sermons*, 235.

back than his or her birth is an orphan. To be human is to be enrolled in a story.

Every person alive is a compilation of multiple crashing, colliding narratives.

We are both the stories we receive and the stories we tell.

If I've learned anything in the ten years I've given to being a public spiritual leader, it is this: Because humans are narrative creatures, our primary orientation in identity is inextricably linked to the narratives that comprise our memories, conversations, and emotional responses. To say it plainly: We are the stories we tell ourselves.

A cursory consideration of modern life in America underscores this point. There are multiple divisions within the current American milieu offering fundamentally different narratives. Northerners scoff at Southern racism as if racism is only a *Southern* problem. Local churches and synagogues wage wars between leadership teams, elder boards, and laity regarding the role of women and gay persons because of generational and interpretive stories undergirding the entire debate. Unspoken stories are the most dangerous. Individual family members who are unable or unwilling to tell truthful memories hold family systems hostage. Scientists and theologians speak two different languages. Muslims are treated as terrorists even though most Muslims are peaceful and honorable people.

We are the stories we tell ourselves. We become the stories we privilege. Flannery O'Connor never wrote, "We are the stories we tell ourselves." She actually said it better. She wrote, "It takes a story to make a story."[2]

It takes a story to make a story. Stories produce *more* stories. How significant is it that Scripture, which the church believes possesses the sacred words of God, comes to us primarily in narrative form (not formulas, doctrinal proofs, or diatribe)? Like a script that is incomplete until it is enacted in daily life—this is the meaning and place of Judaism's Torah and Christianity's New Testament, along with Islam's Qur'an.

Which story are you living?

I had a clear example of this in my own life recently.

My friend Randy is the president of a thriving Christian university. He is one of the most dynamic, creative, hard-working leaders I've ever been around. Over breakfast, he explained why many American Christians have so much fear toward Muslims. He informed me that psychologists used to believe that humans made decisions on two levels: that of emotion and

2. O'Connor, *Mystery and Manners*, 202.

that of logic. Despite the stereotype that women are emotional and men are logical, both actually make choices and decisions based upon emotion.[3]

That was the conventional thinking until about fifteen years ago when brain researchers created a third category. Deeper than emotion, deeper than logic resides *fear*. Fear, long thought to be a strong emotion, is not just *psychological*, it is also *physiological*.

It isn't simply spiritual. Fear alters the physical body too.

When someone cuts you off on the expressway, or when someone insults you—your heritage, religious preference, or core values—you get mad. It goes deep in your bones. When someone slanders your family, spouse, or ethnic origin . . . something happens in you, in your very person. At a molecular level. *DNA*. This is a physiological response.

When conversations about Islam and Christianity come up over coffee, or on a news program or call-in radio show, those conversations are not about emotion or logic. They are first rooted in fear. On both sides. Fear reigns. Fear allows a toxic view of *what might be* to trump the beauty of *what is* and the life-giving potential of *what could be*.

This collective fear is the result of the loss of something precious; it's what happens when we don't know our story. And because we don't know our story, we don't know how to see our world and ourselves; and because we don't know how to see, we don't know who we are; and because we don't know who we are, we don't know how to live. And because we don't know how to live creatively for the betterment of the world, we don't know what to believe and value. By *we*, I mostly mean people who claim the Jesus Story as the definitive story for their life.

Sight.

Identity.

Ethics.

Beliefs and values.

That's how it works. For families, religions, sports, art, music. It's true everywhere you look.

3. See Steimer, "Biology of Fear- and Anxiety-Related Behaviors."

Roots

In Genesis we find a story that tells us how to do all of the above—a sacred text primarily concerned with sight, identity, action, and beliefs.

Abraham found himself in an impossible situation. His beautiful wife, Sarah—whom he had twice attempted to sell in a pinch, out of fear for his own life—was unable to bear him a son. Barrenness, in the ancient world, was not only thought to be a curse from God (or the gods); it was also believed that a woman had not fulfilled her role in a sacred relationship if she was unable to bring her husband the gift of children.

A woman who could not produce a son was expendable.

This married couple was getting older. No children. It was the proverbial elephant in the room at every dinner, the thing each of them thought about but didn't have the nerve to discuss.

Sarah became so frustrated with the entire situation (herself, God, Abraham—maybe her inability to bring children was his fault) that she decided to take matters into her own hands (Gen 16). God promised her husband that God would keep a special relationship with Abraham and all of his descendants, accomplishing God's purposes in the world through a particular people on behalf of the rest of the world.

Just one problem remained. They were still waiting on God. Promises are nice. But promises don't mean anything until they come true. Not only did Abraham lack five children in pursuit of God's promise that his offspring would be too many to count, Abraham lacked one child. Hence, Sarah's decision to orchestrate events is about survival.

Sarah brings *The Help* into the predicament. She has a maidservant from Egypt named Hagar. Sarah knows that if Abraham agrees to conceive a child with Hagar, that son can begin to fulfill the promise of God. At the age of eighty-five, Abraham takes Hagar as his second wife. A year later, Hagar bears a son to Abraham. His name is Ishmael.[4]

During the pregnancy, animosity emerges between the two wives. Sarah, perhaps the most powerful maternal figure in the clan, approaches Abraham, demanding that he do something (16:5). Sarah mistreats Hagar and Hagar flees. While she's on the run, God comes near for the first time in the form of an angel and tells her, "Go back and submit to Sarai and I'll also bless your offspring as I will bless the offspring of Sarai" (16:9–10).[5]

---

4. Admittedly, Hagar is a slave, not a maid. The comparison isn't perfect. But the comparison is worth paying attention to.

5. *Moby Dick* begins with that famous line from its main character, "Call me Ishmael,"

This is the first time in the Bible that an angel is sent to humans. And it's to a slave girl on the margins of society. Calling Ishmael a wild donkey (Gen 16:12) is a compliment; it means he will survive. (So next time you'd like to compliment someone . . .) Up to this point in Genesis, God has named people, but now Hagar names God. She's the Bible's first theologian, and look at what she names Him: *You are the God who sees me.* She has been abused, written off, and cast out, and now she thinks she's just going to die in the wilderness. And it's when she hits rock bottom that she turns around and learns that God is with her; God's watching her.

God essentially says to Hagar, "I know you are a minor character in this drama, but I see you"—for the name of the town near the well where God meets her literally means "to see" or "to be seen," while the name of the well itself means "well of the Living One who sees me." Hagar names God as the one who sees us, all of us. She knows she's on the JV team, but she believes God needs the JV team too. She will do what God has instructed. She will return to live with the rest of the family.

Eighteen months after Ishmael's circumcision, tension erupts between Sarah and Hagar. Sarah gives birth to a miraculous gift from God, Isaac. Hagar continues to deal with all kinds of drama and eventually is divorced, freed, and banished from the family. God spares Ishmael from dying (as God will spare Isaac) by providing water (21:14ff.) at the eleventh hour. Genesis describes two promises given to Hagar and Ishmael: their descendants will multiply, and Ishmael will be the father of a great nation (25:12–18).

Several years following the barbaric attacks carried out by a small, militant Muslim extremist group against targets in New York and Washington, DC—the tragic events of 9/11—it is important to note that *orthodox Islam traces its roots back to Ishmael, while Jews and Christians identify with Isaac.* Approximately 2.2 billion Christians and 1.6 billion Muslims are now a part of the symphony that is the human population of planet Earth (that's 50 percent). More than half the world's people (Jews, Christians, and Muslims) trace their physical and spiritual beginnings to this ancient narrative.

Christians, by virtue of being grafted into the Jewish story, are brothers to Islam and Ishmael, even if we are brothers from another mother. I'm not saying we believe the same things; I'm saying we come from the same

---

because Melville believed, as so many interpreters of Genesis have in the past, that Ishmael's character is primarily the archetype for the man who goes from being the outcast to the survivor. *Moby Dick* was profoundly influenced by the stories in Scripture.

place. We share the same family tree. Most of us simply are not willing to look that far back when constructing our family history.

So, we pause to remember:

"I really only love God as much as the person I love the least" (Dorothy Day).

Because "Jesus would rather go to hell than send his enemies there" (Greg Boyd).

Sarah and Hagar and Isaac and Ishmael couldn't live together. They simply couldn't make it work. One of the questions being asked in this story is, "Is this the way it has to be? Do division, violence, and tension have to be the predominant tenor of life in our modern world?"

It's the question the Scriptures ask after Cain kills Abel, Jacob and Esau fall to pieces, and Joseph enrages his elder brothers. *Is this the way it has to be? Is this how God would have us live? Is this how God sees us?*

An important question brings this story into contemporary experience.

I'm aware that the ages of persons reading this book will vary widely. But I still have to ask. Where were you when Japan bombed Pearl Harbor? Or when Jackie Robinson broke the color barrier? When JFK was shot in Dallas, when NASA landed on the moon, when Elvis shook his hips, when Michael Jackson unveiled the moonwalk? Certain moments define us (nationally and personally)—moments so significant that we can never go back and pretend to be the people we used to be. Where were you when the World Trade Center towers came crashing down on September 11, 2001?

I think often of that dreadful day. *September 11*, or *9-11-01*, has been seared into our country's memory and soul. We are still a nation learning how to grieve. Some of you, like me, have family who have served or are serving in the U.S. military because of what happened on that awful day.

That particular Tuesday began much like any other Tuesday. My morning was mundane: I ate a bowl of cereal, shaved, went to a history survey class, and gathered with friends in a student lounge on the campus of Rochester College in suburban Detroit. I was dressed nicer than usual, which my friends pointed out, because I was going to a funeral. My roommate's great-grandmother, Hattie Mae Robinson, had died the previous week, and a few teammates and coaches were wearing our Sunday best to pay respects to the Robinson family.

We were scheduled to leave Rochester, Michigan, at about 8:45 a.m. for the 9:30 a.m. funeral in downtown Detroit. Walking out of my dorm, I noticed dozens of people gathered around the televisions placed around campus. "What's going on?" I asked rather innocently. "You won't believe it," one student responded. "A plane crashed into one of the towers in Manhattan. The whole thing is on fire."

I didn't have time to process what was being said; I was late for an important funeral. I rode down to Ebenezer Baptist with two close friends. As I jumped into the car, I sensed they were also caught up in the events unfolding in New York City. I heard Peter Jennings' voice, now being listened to by millions of Americans all over the country on television and radio. He kept repeating the phrase, "Oh my God. Oh my God." He wasn't referring to God in the abstract. He was truly lamenting to God, if God existed . . . that God must do something.

During the drive downtown, we learned that a second plane had hit the other WTC tower. Now rumors were swelling, rumors that included words like *war*, *terrorists*, *plot*, *cells*. Needless to say, we did not have time to listen to all the details once we got to the church for the funeral.

This was perhaps one of the most transformative funerals I've ever been a part of. Lament, worship, prayer, confession, and preaching were all a part of the gathering. I do not remember the name of the young minister who stood up to deliver a message that morning, but I owe him a phone call or note of gratitude.

"Did you all hear the news? There was a plane. There was a building. There was a plane and a building . . ." (at that moment someone in the audience shouted "Twin Towers"). "Life is fragile; your decisions matter," the minister reminded us.

I got a little nervous; I know a challenging sermon at a white funeral wouldn't go over well. But he did not relent in his prophetic role as pastor.

Later, the world would learn of the chaos and confusion of the day (e.g., hundreds if not thousands ran toward the water near the Statue of Liberty and returned north just in time for the second tower's collapse), along with the incredible bravery and compassion demonstrated by rescue workers. We would also learn that thirty-one American Muslims died in the terrorist attacks.

But in that moment, the preacher refused to allow his congregation to pretend that evil did not exist within his flock just because evil was so visible in the destruction wrought in New York.

"You all come up in here acting religious. But I know some of y'all. You come up in here when I know where you been last night. You been drinkin', smokin', . . . having sex."

No way could I get away with this at a white funeral.

As God is my witness, when he said "drinkin' . . . smokin' . . . having sex," the organist struck the keys at just the right moment, creating an effect on the human spirit rarely felt in most white churches. I didn't know if I'd done anything wrong the weekend before, but I was ready to repent.

He was doing the moonwalk . . . can you see it?

Immediately following, a beautiful young black woman sang "His Eye Is on the Sparrow"—and there it was, the Gospel of Jesus: acknowledgment of evil, judgment of sins, hope everlasting.

As I left the funeral and drove back home that morning, I had this overwhelming sense that my world had changed. More importantly, our *world* had changed. It was a deep knowing in my gut that went beyond intellectual awareness. At least now I had some categories for the lament I'd experienced while reading the Psalms and the disconnect in churches whose mission seemed to be making people feel good about themselves. Some thinkers call this "moralistic therapeutic deism."[6] It means we turn God into a cosmic vending machine, only consulting the divine when there's something in it for us. I'm not sure what that all entails but I think they're onto something.

This is why I'm writing this book, telling this story, creating this conversation.

The fundamental challenge of visionary leadership—be it in local churches, schools, businesses, synagogues, mosques, or organizations—is not getting everyone to believe the right things, nor is it to get everyone to have the same specific passions for justice. The fundamental challenge of leadership is to instill and cultivate a prophetic imagination. After all, doctrine and work won't move us further into the kingdom. It's not about believing or doing. It's about sight. Can we see as Jesus saw?

Imagination is more important than doctrine or action. Imagination is the soil that produces certain beliefs and practices.

Can we see our Muslim neighbors? Do we see Muslims *as* neighbors? That's a lot to digest. Pause. Breathe. Pause. Breathe. Repeat.

One of my professors in graduate school, the acclaimed writer and speaker Barbara Brown Taylor, tells the story of a student who had a tattoo that simply read, "And." When Taylor saw the tattoo after class, she asked her student, "And? And what?"

---

6. See Smith and Denton, *Soul Searching*.

"Oh, this?" the student said, pointing to her tattoo. "It's part of an experiment. Actually, a *living* novel project."

"Huh," responded Taylor.

"Many of us have the same favorite author. He created the living novel project. He's recruiting people to take one word and tattoo it on their body."

"And this means something to you?" Taylor asked.

"Yes. It means a lot. I don't have to bear the whole story. I just have to bear one word." Taylor goes on to say that she loves the idea of God as this particular author. The author looks around, knowing he's given each person one word. Just one word to bear before the world's eyes.

What's *your* word? What's *your* phrase? That's a question worth pausing to consider. What's the word you bring to the narrative God is writing in the midst of the human networks you belong? *How* Not *to Kill a Muslim* is part of the discovery process.

I'll never forget Dr. Loren Siffring telling me, as a sophomore in college, over French toast and chocolate milk, that my identity was "seeker of truth." "That's who you are, Josh," he said. "You can't do anything to change it."

I've been seeking God ever since. The truth is I was seeking God all along. Theologically stated: God was seeking me and I simply responded.

One cannot overestimate how important it is for a young man to be spoken to in that way. I think this is how God works. I think this is how we appropriate Jesus in our cities. It takes a story to make a story. We are the stories we tell ourselves.

It's true in Genesis. It's true in North America and the U.S. It's true in the Middle East. It's true in Islam. It's true in Christianity. *If Christianity is of Christ, that is*. Truth-telling and the power of story. Life depends upon this.

The Bible sets in motion a trajectory we often ignore. The trajectory—stripped of superfluous language—can be summarized: You are better than this.

Have you ever noticed the development of sibling relationship in the Genesis narrative? The younger brother always supplants, overthrows the elder brother. In a culture based on honor and shame, land rights, and family authority, this would be hard to swallow for listeners and readers.

In Genesis, there is constant tension between older and younger—and you always have to watch out for the younger brother. Cain kills Abel. Isaac, the younger brother, and Ishmael live in noticeable tension because they know their family story. Jacob, the younger brother, steals Esau's birthright. Eventually they reconcile. Joseph's older brothers sell him into slavery. He rises to power through incredible circumstances. He has the chance to crush his brothers but instead welcomes them with hospitality and undeserved love.

And Exodus joins the fun. Exodus begins with the story of Moses, the younger brother of Aaron and Miriam (Exod 7:7; Aaron is three years older than Moses). The elder brother is a supporter of Moses—God's reluctant mouthpiece. The elder brother will see God's purposes unfold. And because God loves to keep us sharp, he also reminds us that the siblings in the family aren't just boys. *Miriam is now part of the plot too.* Try to find another ancient religious text that has this kind of chutzpah.

It's like Genesis and Exodus are saying that there is often tension between family members, between communities, between religious sects, but that doesn't mean that it has to be this way. Just as my generation has been hard on previous generations for their treatment of African-Americans, my children will judge me on my treatment of Muslims.

It doesn't have to be like *this.*

Isaac doesn't have to pretend to be Ishmael. Ishmael doesn't have to pretend to be Isaac. But if Isaac really trusts God, he will strive to be the best son he knows how to be, challenging Ishmael to be the best son he can be, and, in the end, we trust God to work through us, to sort out the family mess that began so many generations ago.

If it's true that we are the stories we tell ourselves . . . we need better stories. But first, we need to see the chaos created by our bad stories.

I'm a *Jesus person.* I want everyone to be a *Jesus person.* This is what it looks like to be a *Jesus person* for those who are not *Jesus people.*

2

When Crescent and Cross Collide

> If the God you believe in hates all the same people you do,
> then you know you've created God in your own image.[1]

ESTIMATED TO REPRESENT SOME seventy million adherents, evangelical Christianity in North America has made enemies within four specific groups: Muslims, gays and lesbians (LGBTQ), political opponents (generally speaking, those who lean *left*), and the economically disenfranchised. Recent courage and creativity in ministry in many local Christian congregations has led many practical theologians to conclude that evangelical Christian communities are doing an admirable job establishing ties with the latter but struggling mightily concerning the first three.

It is the assumption of this book that the relationship between American Muslims and American Christians is a most pressing issue. A few basic questions guide this conversation: How might leaders within local communities of faith embrace an appreciative and informed view of the Islamic faith in general and American Muslims in particular? How might we learn to love and see American Muslims as our neighbors? What practices and attitudes might emerge from such an exploration?

This project is primarily focused on the relationship and responsibility of Christians toward Muslims within the context of urban centers (like

---

1. Lamott, *Bird by Bird*, 22.

where I live: Nashville). In this chapter, I explore the cultural and religious biases embedded within Protestant evangelical Christianity and highlight strategies for dialogue, appreciation, understanding, and shared ministry between Christians and Muslims living in the United States.

The following chapters will not explore politics or the categories created by our fixation with the *right* (or *conservatives*) versus the *left* (or *liberals*). My goal is to reclaim a more biblical *missional* ecclesiology: to help Christian people see, think, and act as Jesus *actually* saw, thought, and acted. I want to name, expose, challenge, and transform the stereotypes and attitudes of Christians, and especially evangelical Christians in America, toward Muslims.

As I've already mentioned, Muslims (1.6 billion) and Christians (2.2 billion) make up nearly half the world's population. These numbers are indicative of a growing competition between Muslims and Christians. As one observer of the tension writes, "Islam and Christianity are again rivals, competing cheek by jowl for people, power, and public opinion."[2] Contrary to popular belief in Europe and the U.S., the majority of Muslims around the world are *not* Arab-speaking Middle Easterners. Eighty percent of all Muslims in the world do not speak an Arabic language or live in the Middle East. While misleading impressions suggest otherwise, many Muslims live in Africa, Indonesia, and India.

Over the last one hundred years the number of Christians has declined from 35 to 32 percent of the world's population. In that same span, Islam has grown from 12 percent to 22 percent. Many scholars believe that Islam is growing 33 percent faster than Christianity.

The U.S. has a Muslim population of roughly 4 to 7 million, which is less than 2 percent of our total population of 310 to 325 million. There are more Detroit Tigers fans living in the U.S. than Muslims. (Who are the Detroit Tigers? *Exactly*.) However, it has been estimated that the number of Muslims in the United States could double in the next twenty to twenty-five years.[3]

As a result of the Immigration and Nationality Act of 1965, which allowed people from all over the world—not just Europeans—to enter and

2. Prothero, *God Is Not One*, 97.

3. See Grossman, "Numbers of U.S. Muslims to Double." While I'm looking at the current and future immigration patterns of Muslims in the United States and North America, it's critical to remember that Muslims have been part of the American experiment—and population explosion—from this nation's very inception. See, for example, Manseau, "The Muslims of Early America."

become citizens of the U.S., our country has witnessed a dramatic increase in the influence of other languages, faiths, and values—what is classically called *culture*. We are immensely and intensely *multi*-cultural. Many languages. Many faiths. Many values. Many stories. All thrown into this mixing bowl we call *America*.

While it might be fair to suggest that many Muslims around the world are suspicious of the West (on issues such as lax morality, past warfare, sexual ethics), it is grossly unfair to suggest that a billion-plus people are inherently violent, hateful, sinister, and anti-American. The terrorist attacks of 9/11 in New York City, Washington DC, and Pennsylvania were funded and executed by a small extremist segment of the Muslim population. However, the events were not sanctioned Muslim attacks upon Christian America. Some Muslims cheered the collapse of the twin towers, but many Muslims grieved the sheer horror of 9/11, knowing that it would set back relations between Christians and Muslims at least fifty years. More than sixty Muslims died on that fateful September day. Imam Mohammed, spiritual leader of the 12th Avenue *masjid* in Nashville (Nashville's largest Muslim intentional community), recently said to me, "9/11 was one of the darkest days of my life. I knew my experience in the United States would never be the same." He not only mourned the dead, he mourned the death of budding interfaith friendships. He mourned the agony and painful rise of stereotypes that would certainly cause harm in a post-9/11 climate of fear, mistrust, and outright hate.

Because this book is mostly directed at people who consider themselves, in thought and practice, disciples of the teachings of Jesus, I offer the following observation. There are at least four basic convictions I bring to this book regarding the local context in which I live and for whom I write. I suspect the following working assumptions are true for your context.

First assumption: Many Christians live such busy lives—caring for children, pursuing education, and working hard—that this entire subject is remarkably intimidating because their *margin for deep reflection is limited at best*. Let's be honest: after work, family, and—finally—some rest . . . who has the time to think about "saving the world" or the "plight of Muslims in America"? Most of us would admit, *The last thing I want to think about after a long day is the future of the entire planet. No thanks. I'll settle for* Modern Family. But I'm not alone in thinking that the most important global/local (what some fashionably refer to as *glocal*) issue of the twenty-first century is the collision of Christianity with Islam in various hot spots around the world: Western Europe, Africa, and the United States, to name three obvious examples. And we Christians, no matter how busy our lives become, would do well both to acknowledge the issue and to act.

Second assumption: A large number of Christians are *bitter toward Muslims* because they don't know any Muslims. In the absence of authentic relationships, 9/11 provides an unhealthy narrative regarding "those Muslims we can't trust."[4] That is, many Christians are afraid of Muslims because Christians lack authentic, deep relationship with them. This is a familiar sociological pattern in Christian history. The marginalization of Jews, gay persons, the homeless, ethnic minorities, etc., is common in mainstream WASP America or mainstream *white* Western Christianity.

This is the *principle of distance* or *proximity*. The less relational knowledge and experience I have about a particular group of people or a specific person the less inherent empathy I have for that person. This is a large problem in America particularly because of our remarkable commitment to diversity, inclusive immigration policies, and so forth. We invite the entire world to enter our borders and then don't know what to do once the world takes us up on our offer. When persons of other faiths and ethnicities come to the U.S. and don't become *just like us* (and by *us*, white people usually mean *white people*, that is, *us* = *white*), we intuitively make people *other* people. We *other* them—that is, we create distance betwen *us* and *them* with our attitudes, speech, stereotypes, jokes, and action.

Third assumption: *The majority of American Christians have fallen for dangerous stereotypes* propagated within most segments of pop culture: film, stories, news, music, talk radio, television. We create and accept caricatures of Muslims as backwards, evil, violent, sinister, and deceitful. Again, the terrorist attacks of militant Muslims on 9/11 have been the chief source of this angst and confusion. We default to caricatures from pop culture that are, in a word, false.

Fourth assumption: *Many Christians feel completely underequipped in engaging persons of different faiths* (Buddhists, Hindus, or Baha'is, but especially Muslims). The entire issue feels like a giant mountain that cannot be climbed by the average person. We'd rather watch *Downton Abbey* or

---

4. In actuality, the majority of Muslims do not support or advocate the use of violence—a fact borne out by a 2013 report issued by the Pew Forum on Religion & Public Life that found that "few Muslims endorse suicide bombing and other forms of violence against civilian targets as a means of defending Islam against its enemies" ("The World's Muslims," 70). Despite this fact, Christians continue to tell themselves a story about Muslims that simply isn't true.

update our iPhones—those tasks seem *doable*, whereas interfaith dialogue and engagement require so much effort with unclear, if any, payoffs.

As a *Christian* leader, writer, and minister, I fervently hope all people—including Christians and Muslims—come to experience the power of Jesus' teachings, life, death, and resurrection; I hope they become what the New Testament describes as people of the Way (Acts 19:23). I am, in a sense, unapologetically Christian. But I've come to believe that unapologetic Christianity should be a source of intrigue and interest to persons of other faiths.

A focal point emerges in my mind. That is, this entire conversation funnels to a few fundamental questions. Did Jesus die for Christians or did Jesus die for everyone, for all of his enemies? If Jesus' life is the model for the Christian life, what does it mean then to be willing to die for those who do not share our Christian language, values, and stories (cf. 2 Cor 5)? How might our good news be good news for everyone? Kwame Bediako, African theologian *par excellence*, frames it this way in thinking about his own continent of Africa:

> In other words, our Christian affirmations about the uniqueness of Christ achieve their real impact when they are subjected to the test to establish their credentials and validity not only in terms of the religious and spiritual universe in which Christians habitually operate, but also and indeed especially, in terms of the religious and spiritual worlds which persons of other faiths inhabit.[5]

That is, the real test of Christianity's truth is whether or not it can provide life and hope for those who do not subscribe to Christianity as true. I ponder this question often: What if the church in North America earned a reputation for being first responders to the complexities of new faiths coming into the U.S. over the next fifteen years, as opposed to being portrayed as angry, fearful, or indifferent? What if evangelical churches were able to shorten the time gap of understanding, appreciation, and inclusion of minority groups—African-Americans from 1860 to 1965, for instance—which we so often fail to see as the work of God in our midst? I think that would be, in a word, *kingdom*. Or, in the spirit of Dag Hammarskjöld: *It is truly more for one to labor totally for one individual than to work fervently for the salvation of the masses.*

As it relates to our Muslim neighbors in North America, we must not put the cause over the individual. Jesus was not merely referring to a group

5. Bediako, *Jesus and the Gospel in Africa*, 37.

when he told the story of the Good Samaritan—he was talking about a real person. My caution is that we get so caught up in the cause that we lose sight of the person, and when we do that we fail both the person and the cause. Our first responsibility is to the person. However, this is not an either/or option; it is a *both/and*, but with a priority that I believe is word and deed of the Jesus Creed. We start with the person nearest (both yourself and the neighbor) and the cause then begins to make more sense.

Christians cannot love groups of people; we can only love the person right in front of us. We cannot love groups of people; we can only love people. We can only love people by loving one person at a time. We must do for one what we wish we could do for everyone.

Let's get particular.

3

"All Muslims Are Terrorists!"

BEFORE YOU READ ANY further in this book . . . stop.

Seriously. Pause. Take a deep breath. Doesn't that feel good?

Now take out a pen and paper (or iPhone notepad, or Evernote, or use the margin of this book) and, for three minutes, write down *all* the words, images, thoughts, and stories that come to your mind when you read the words in the bulleted list below. Don't critique yourself. Just write whatever's in you. Have a spouse or friend or neighbor do this too.

- Muslim . . .
- Middle Easterner . . .
- Allah . . .
- Iran . . . Afghanistan . . .
- Saddaam Hussein . . .
- The Koran (Qur'an) . . . Shari'ah law . . .
- September 11, 2001 . . .
- Terrorists . . . Jihad . . . Suicide bombers . . .
- Submission . . .

- Osama bin Laden . . .

Now, look back at your answers. Do any of them surprise you? What words or images emerged? Would you want others to read your responses?

Once you've done this, keep reading.

Did you do it? Did you tell the truth?

North American Muslims and Christians are suspicious of each other. Fear, suspicion, distrust, and callousness color the conversation. Christians and Muslims must continue the task of knowing each other in order to value each other and live together peaceably. And to do so, Christians must confront the stereotypes that are the projections of our own personal fears and not the reality of those we have dehumanized.

The most uninformed have no difficulty identifying the Muslim portrayed in cartoon form. He is the one with sinister, squinty eyes, large nose, and *kafiyya* (Arab headdress), rubbing his hands together and asking where he can get a pickup truck and a homemade bomb. Or standing with a sign that reads, *Death to all American infidels* next to a minister whose sign reads, *Pray for peace.* Or pointing to a chart that targets Manhattan, nursery schools, nursing homes, and maternity wards, and asking whether there are other nominations before the vote on which to bomb first.

Perhaps the greatest challenge facing religious leaders seeking to bring Christians and Muslims to a deeper understanding of each other's faith is the formidable stereotypes that have taken deep root in the imaginations of the American Christian and Muslim. Jesus' half-brother, James, once wrote, "With the tongue we praise our Lord and Father, and with it *we curse people who have been made in God's likeness*" (Jas 3:9). John Barton highlights the problem:

> Muslim/Christian interactions are often about as rational and helpful as what is depicted in the comedy routine between Steve Carell and Stephen Colbert on the *Daily Show* in which they argue over which religion is better. Like all good comedy, this piece entertains while it delivers a sharp indictment. It mocks the inappropriate ways Christians and Muslims often employ apologetics or *power encounter* tactics; it belies assumptions that Christian/Muslim interactions must involve political positioning and debates over superiority, or that the primary purpose of interactions is to address conflicting visions of salvation. It also playfully critiques the idea that the only Christian/Muslim alliances that are possible are those built on the shared mistrust of a common opponent (e.g., Jews). As Christians, we need to promote a different posture for

Christian reflection and *missional* engagement with Islam and our Muslim neighbors.[1]

So go the stereotypes: the Christian is a wealthy, upper-middle-class white man who loves war, women, beer, NFL football, edgy comedy, fast food and even faster cars. The Muslim is the poor, illiterate, angry simpleton who hates freedom, treats his wife harshly, and longs for the day when the United States becomes a fully Muslim nation by way of Shari'ah law. While the previous might be alarmist, it captures prevailing stereotypes. According to the Council on American-Islamic Relations (CAIR), American Muslims face daunting stereotypes in the country of their citizenship. "Although coverage of Islam has increased in the past few years, many Muslims believe their faith continues to be misunderstood," states a guide to understanding Islam and Muslims issued by CAIR in 2007. "Like people of other faiths, Muslims cannot be described in simple or monolithic terms. There are no easy, one-size-fits-all answers for this growing and dynamic community."[2]

Think about it. When was the last time you read a book, watched a movie, or enjoyed a TV program in which a Muslim character was portrayed as honest, virtuous, or heroic? As I was rewriting this chapter, a well-known musician tweeted the following (you couldn't make this stuff up):

No wonder middle east countries are hard to get along with

No NASCAR

No Football

No alcohol

No country music

And they don't eat pork chops[3]

Fear, the genesis of misunderstanding, sells. In buckets and buckets . . . it sells. *Fear is big business.* Don't believe me? Just watch Fox News or CNN. CAIR reports that negative images of Muslims were sixteen times more

1. Barton, "Missional Posture," para. 3.

2. CAIR, *American Muslims*, 7. The results of my survey at Otter Creek Church of Christ confirm these findings; see Appendix III. Of course, the division between who is American and who is Christian is a difficult point of delineation in this kind of research.

3. Charlie Daniels, Twitter post, May 18, 2014, https://twitter.com/CharlieDaniels/status/468187316310142976. Also, I have no idea why *football* is capitalized.

pervasive than positive images.[4] About one in four Americans believes in anti-Muslim canards (e.g., Muslims teach their children to hate, and they value life less than other people). Those with the most negative attitudes toward Muslims tend to be male, white, less educated, politically conservative, Republican Party members, living in the Southern region (of course, the chances of this population actually knowing any Muslims are slim). When asked what comes to mind when they hear the word *Muslim*, 32 percent made negative comments; only 2 percent had a positive response. A 2006 *Washington Post-ABC News* poll uncovered that 46 percent of Americans have a negative view of Islam. This same study also found that 25 percent of Americans admitted to harboring prejudice toward Muslims.[5] It is important to note that people's viewpoints are generally worse in reality than what they are even willing to report for a study. These numbers are disturbing.

Robert Wuthnow, American sociologist and ethnographer, confirms CAIR's findings. In his landmark book, *America and the Challenges of Religious Diversity,* he captures some of the troubling attitudes of conservative Christians toward Muslims in America. Here are the pertinent stats for our purposes:

55 percent believe that Muslims are fanatical.

52 percent believe that Muslims are violent.

66 percent believe that Muslims are closed-minded.

58 percent believe that Muslims are strange.

Only 26 percent believe that Muslims are peace-loving.

55 percent indicated that they do not want the Muslim population to increase (whatsoever) in the United States.

79 percent stated they would object to one of their children marrying a Muslim with a good education from a good home.

62 percent noted they would not support a mosque built in their community.[6]

---

4. CAIR, *American Muslims*, 46.

5. See Deane and Fears, "Negative Perceptioin of Islam Increasing," paras. 2 and 6.

6. Wuthnow, *America and the Challenges*, 56ff. In this section I'm quoting stats from Wuthnow's heading "Christian Exclusivists" (i.e., conservative Christians). See the results of the surveys I gave at Otter Creek Church in Appendix III.

The Accident of Birth

Approximately three to seven million Muslims live in the United States. According to Wuthnow, "About two-thirds of Muslims in America are immigrants and their descendants, the majority of which, contrary to popular belief, did not come from the Middle East, but from Pakistan, India, Bangladesh, Indonesia, Africa and elsewhere; most of the remainder were African Americans."[7] At the turn of the twenty-first century, Muslims worshiped in approximately three thousand centers, mosques, and prayer locations, and had established roughly two hundred Muslim schools.[8]

When and how did we get to this point? When and how did Islam become an important part of the fabric of American society?

A basic working knowledge regarding the genesis of religious pluralism is vital. This entire discussion leads back to shifting U.S. immigration policies dating back as recently as 1965.

I will not soon forget a certain political cartoon from *USA Today* some years ago. The picture depicted two Native Americans walking behind a campfire. Sitting at the campfire were two male pilgrims dressed in full period regalia. The pilgrims were cleaning an animal recently killed. As the two pilgrims prepared their evening meal, one Native American looked back toward the other with a wry smile, saying, "I wish those illegal immigrants would go back to *where they came from.*"

The cartoonist's point is the same point that Malcolm X famously made when he said, "We didn't land on Plymouth Rock. Plymouth Rock landed on us." Or when, in a speech I attended at a local university in Metro Detroit, Spike Lee asked a question concerning the traditional retelling of Christopher Columbus's discoveries: "How can you discover a place in which people already live?" The real history of population, habitation, religious diversity, and immigration is sordid, messy, and complicated. Christians need to ask good questions because good questions are usually critical to complex issues.

History is almost always written from the comfort of privileged social location. Wherever one finds oneself on the issue of immigration (and it seems there are very few people who lack an opinion on the subject), seeing the discussion on a slant is significant for deeper understanding. That is, the subject needs to be assessed from all different perspectives.

7. Ibid., 216–19.
8. Ibid., 57.

Immigration and religious diversity, sibling issues that cannot be separated in American history or current debate, are two of the most divisive issues facing America today. An elementary understanding of the history of immigration and religious diversity in the United States as shaped by the (brilliantly conceived) First Amendment is paramount for persons of faith to have constructive language as they navigate the chaotic waters of religious diversity, zoning, interfaith dialogue, etc.

Immigration in the United States changed forever in 1965. For more than half a century prior, U.S. law made it virtually impossible for non-Europeans to immigrate to the land of the capitalist and the home of the WASP. In the 1920s, the U.S. had adopted an immigration ideology based on a model that empowered government officials to discriminate on the basis of ethnicity, political question marks, and religion.

In 1965, everything changed. That year, the Immigration and Nationality Act (named the Hart-Celler Act for its cosponsors) passed, though it would not be fully implemented until July 1968. This piece of legislation "quietly flung our demographic doors open to all of the world's religions," writes Krista Tippett.[9] This piece of legislation essentially shifted the major criteria for immigration acceptance from nationality and political ideology to family connections, sponsorship potential, and skill or education status. The doors of opportunity were no longer held open for European lovers of democracy only, but for all of those seeking a better life.

The controversial bill was proposed by U.S. Representative Emanuel Celler (NY), cosponsored by U.S. Senator Philip Hart (MI), and heavily supported by Senator Ted Kennedy (MA). It allowed for approximately three hundred thousand visas to be granted annually to immigrants: one hundred seventy thousand reserved for citizens of eastern hemisphere countries, and the remaining for citizens of countries in the western hemisphere. The bill passed 329–79 in the House of Representatives and 76–18 in the Senate.

Between 1965 and 1970, the number of immigrants living in the U.S. doubled. This number doubled again between 1970 and 1990. The Immigration and Nationality Act of 1965 altered the racial narrative of the U.S. to an extent never seen before. In the 1950s, for instance, 53 percent of immigrants were European, with only 6 percent being Asian. By the 1990s, only 16 percent of immigrants came from Europe, while 31 percent came from Asia. The result: today the United States is the most religiously, ethnically,

9. Tippett, *Speaking of Faith*, 4.

culturally, and economically diverse nation in the world, and probably the most diverse nation in history. Immigration policies have opened the door of opportunity to people of all religious backgrounds, including Muslims. Their influx is not going to slow down anytime soon.

Though a proponent of the act, President Lyndon Johnson could not have been more wrong when he predicted that "this bill we sign today is not a revolutionary bill. It does not affect the lives of millions. It will not restructure the shape of our daily lives."[10] Temples, mosques, *masjids* would now become part of the urban scene—right next to churches, schools, and restaurants.

Proximity isn't what it used to be.

Johnson's predecessor, John F. Kennedy, better understood the significance of the bill. For JFK, this was an ideological move. In the shadow of older immigration policy and the pending proposals that eventually became the Immigration and Nationality Act of 1965, JFK said that a national origins system "neither satisfies a national need nor accomplishes an international purpose. In an age of interdependence among nations, such a system is an anachronism, for it discriminates among applicants for admission into the United States on the basis of the accident of birth."[11] While the U.S. Declaration of Independence asserts that all "men are created equal," it has taken some time for the doors of opportunity to open to *all* men and *all* women. Now that this is happening, all people (citizens and noncitizens) are bringing with them their faiths, cultures, values, and beliefs—their most important possessions.

Prior to the 1960s America saw itself primarily as a nation comprised of Protestants, Catholics, and Jews. Immigration forced these three groups to move over and make room for Hindus, Sikhs, Muslims, and Buddhists, as well as a host of other ethnic-religious communities. More room was needed at the proverbial table of citizenship. The 2010 American Community Survey confirms this: The foreign-born population of the U.S. then was 40 million (12.9 percent of the total U.S. population). Between 2009 and 2010, the foreign-born population increased by 1.4 million people. Fifty-three percent of all foreign-born residents were from Latin America. The single largest country-of-birth group, Mexico, represented 29 percent of

10. Johnson spoke these words on October 3, 1965, the day he signed the Immigration and Nationality Act into law. Quoted in Hammer and Safi, *Cambridge Companion to American Islam*, 65.

11. Address to Congress, July 23, 1963. Quoted in Kennedy, *Nation of Immigrants*, Appendix D, "Major Immigration Policy Developments."

all foreign born. The foreign born from Asia represented 28 percent of all foreign born in 2010; the foreign born from Europe represented 12 percent; and the foreign born from Africa represented 4 percent.[12]

As a *direct* result of America's long-standing policy of inclusive immigration, imperfect though it may be, citizens of this country, especially Christians, must deal with the reality that the U.S. will continue to have the most diverse religious population of any country in the world. The church desperately needs a theological framework for engagement with persons from diverse backgrounds lest we defer to the strategies of political parties. When this happens, the church's witness and power are neutered. *Evangelical* Christians, if that name means *anything* at all, should assume the role of catalyst and bear the marks and message of God's kingdom—the focus of the next section—alive in the life of Jesus. That is, Christians have an opportunity at this very moment to lead the way on dialogue and reconciliation and resist taking our cues from the broader American culture and its talking heads on cable news and radio, who dispense fear, paranoia, misinformation, hatred, and suspicion. Stephen Prothero reminds us how crucial this conversation is for the present and, more importantly, for the *future*:

> One of the great challenges of this increasingly global church is how to reckon with its Muslim neighbors. For most of Christian history, Jews were the Christians' closest conversations partners. Christianity was from the beginning an amalgamation of Hellenistic and Hebraic influences and just how the two should be mixed has always stirred contention. But today Christianity and Islam are the world's greatest religions. Together Christians and Muslims account for roughly half of the world's population, and for more than half of the world's suicide bombers and drone attacks.[13]

Let's catch our breath. Up to this point, we've explored the problem with stereotypes, the basic narrative of immigration, and the diversity of our nation. It's now time to turn to the brilliant, world-shattering teachings of Jesus. To paraphrase Dallas Willard, it's not enough to say that Jesus is Lord or Son of God; it is also possible (though not provable) that, on matters of life and faith, Jesus is the smartest and wisest human being in the history of the world.

---

12. 2010 American Community Survey Highlights, 1, https://www.census.gov/newsroom/releases/pdf/acs_2010_highlights.pdf.

13. Prothero, *God Is Not One*, 96.

The center of orthodox Christian theology and practice is the life Jesus actually led. When you don't know where to start, Jesus is the best place. When you are lost, go back to the place you last knew where you were and start from there. For me, that always means I turn back to the life and energy of Jesus.

He never disappoints.

4

The Heart of the Jesus Story

"FAITH IS THE ENDURING ability to *imagine* life in a certain way," claims James Whitehead.[1] If Whitehead is right, Christians have a unique opportunity at this juncture in history to imagine our faith intersecting with the faiths of others in new and fresh ways. Christianity, like Judaism, is a faith built upon contextual and progressive revelation. Christians do not believe that God uses Scripture one time, in one way, for one purpose. Christians believe God uses Scripture to speak fresh words, into new situations, for unimagined outcomes. If Acts 17:26–27 is accurate—that God is involved in the lives, the "existence and boundaries," of various people groups—the church must be poised to think carefully about how we respond to the shifting contours of our communities and the manner in which we engage a diversity of religious beliefs and practices.

But before we do so, we need to properly frame the world Jesus entered in order to fully appreciate *how* Jesus entered said world. Only after those two pieces are put together might we begin to understand a response to tension, violence, and religious difference in the twenty-first century.

Many Jews in the first century were asking the same questions progressive and traditional Western Christians are pondering today: What does it

---

1. Whitehead, "The Religious Imagination," quoted in Taylor, *Preaching Life*, 44.

26

mean to be the faithful people of God? What must take place in order for God to send his Messiah a second time (evangelical)? What does it look like to fuse the Jesus Way in contemporary society regarding churches, institutions, immigration, and interfaith work (liberal)? The answers offered in the first century were all over the map. Remember, the task of the catholic church is to provide twenty-first-century answers to first-century questions, not nineteenth-century answers (liberalism and fundamentalism) to sixteenth-century questions.

Here's how this worked in Jesus' context.

The Pharisees, an admittedly complex and important group interested in justice and compassion, are depicted in the gospels as religious leaders who tended to reduce religion to matters of private and public purity—this will become important as we survey key texts in which Jesus' mode of operation directly subverts this strategy (e.g., Luke 10:25–37). The Pharisees were committed to the ideal of purity, and that often caused them to clash with Jesus' notion that people were more important than pious principles. This commitment to textual and ethical purity leads one to believe that Pharisees, according to N. T. Wright, "are the individual analogue to the national fear of, and/or resistance to, contamination from, or oppression by, Gentiles."[2] It seems the Pharisees wanted to clean things up and create a morally pure society: *Let's get rid of the homeless, the tax collectors, and the prostitutes* (cf. Matt 5–7; 12:1ff.; 15:1ff.; 16:5; 21:12–15, 23; Luke 12:1–3; John 9). Their passion was pure, their motives God-honoring. But, as we often see today in hypermoralistic strands of the Christian faith, the Pharisees put principles over people, law over love. Not because they thought that obeying rules or keeping principles earned *favor with God*—they were, strictly speaking, people who took *election* and *covenant* very seriously—but because they believed that the rules and regulations were a matter of ushering in the kingdom of God in such a way that God would have the space to definitely show up (in the temple) and end, once and for all, the oppressive and pagan Roman occupation. This was not only a matter of life and death, it was a matter of identity and eschatology. That is, the future of Israel and the world depended upon their faithfulness and devotion to the proper application of Torah.

The Essenes—think here of the Amish in American society—insisted that some righteous ones must withdraw, for all of Jerusalem was corrupt: *We should isolate ourselves from everyone else and create a pure society, a*

---

2. Wright, *New Testament and the People of God*, 188. While he summarizes this *historical grid* in multiple works, this one is probably the most comprehensive.

holy fortress. (Josephus mentions this group in three works: *The Jewish War, Antiquities,* and *The Life of Flavius Josephus.*). Rather than choosing the strategy of control and purity (the Pharisees' option), the Essenes—and other versions of separatist approaches—sought to isolate themselves so that the distractions of a compromised Jerusalem might be muted long enough for a small band of faithful sisters and brothers to become who God intended them to be. The Christian monasteries in the Catholic Church find their spiritual roots in these separatist movements. One succinct way to think about the Essenes: they were essentially Pharisees who sought to live a more ascetic life.

There were other groups.

The Zealots said, *Get your tanks, guns, knives, and planes—we're going to war. Then God will surely intervene* (Luke 9:51–56; John 6:15). They believed (and could cite many Torah texts to support their claims) that violence was the central way to usher in YHWH's redemption of Israel over against the Roman Occupation. Even a cursory reading of the Gospels produces a sense that violence is the norm in the first-century world— among Jews and Romans alike. One of the unique contributions of Jesus in human history is the idea that nonviolent public subversion is a viable strategy in accomplishing communal religious aims (an idea adopted by the Anabaptists, Tolstoy, Thoreau, Gandhi, Martin Luther King Jr.). Jesus proved, in essence, that love willing to suffer on behalf of others (friends, strangers, and even enemies) could do something in and for the world that other strategies could not. So it must have been a sticking point with Jesus' disciples—Peter, James, and John—that at no point does Jesus even hint that violent rebellion is part of the strategy by which he will bring *heaven to earth* as promised in the Matt 6 version of the Lord's Prayer.

The Herodians, Sadducees, and Samaritans were disillusioned by the discussion and their options: *If you can't beat 'em, join 'em. We don't mind sleeping with the enemy* (i.e., Rome; see Mark 3:6; 12:18–27; Luke 20:27–40; John 4; Acts 4:1–3; 23:8). Essentially, these groups, worthy of much further consideration, were accomodationists at their center.

The Pharisees desired to control and purify.

The Essenes desired to separate and purify.

The Zealots desired to win through the power of violence.

Others simply wanted the good life, the first-century version of the American Dream.

The poor, of course, were simply trying to survive.

This is not history *only*. This is theology and philosophy. This is happening today.

This historical grid I've sketched out becomes a compelling contemporary grid. One can create a moral society based upon a fragmented and reductionistic ethical code (the Pharisees' option). Or one can seek to create a radical community completely separate from the rest of the world (the Essenes' option). Or one can declare war on the empire, which, of course, was the Zealots' option. Finally, one can buy wholesale what the empire serves up (the Sadducees' option). Though all of these options show up in modern Christian epistemology and praxis, I choose the Jesus option: incarnation. In this option, claims theologian John Howard Yoder, Christians enter into the complexity, diversity, suffering, and chaos of the world, while maintaining a holy disposition by the power of God's Spirit (John 1; Acts 2, 15; Phil 2:1–11).[3] The incarnation option is radical trust that God will take our skin, sweat, tears, prayers, conversations, and acts of service and draw people closer to God's own heart just as Jesus did. That is, the church will be for the world what Jesus was for Israel. Word moves to flesh. Truth becomes skin. Heaven becomes human. Say it however you want, say what you will about Christianity, it has always been a movement based upon the most ordinary things: water, bread, wine, people, conflict, hope, sacrifice, the future.

By intentionally seeing, teaching, and living in a different way, a countercultural ethic that knew much of religious and ethnic conflict, Jesus provides *a way* (the reason Christianity was referred to as the Way before it was accepted as an official religion)—a way forward for all people, not just people of faith, in the midst of tension between Muslims and Christians and the various nations these two super-religions represent.

We now turn our attention to one of the central texts in Jesus' public teaching ministry—a text that has stood the test of time, transforming entire nations and civilizations. This text is not only the heart of the gospels; it is the heart of all Christian strategy as the church seeks to enter God's world (what some call evangelism, works of mercy, etc.).

The parable of the Merciful Samaritan (Luke 10:25–37) should provide the paradigmatic lens for Christian leaders to participate in dialogue, shared ministry, and deep appreciation for our American Muslim neighbors. If taken seriously, this one biblical text would revolutionize the way we see, live, act, and think. Christians would begin to view their Muslim neighbors with new eyes.

---

3. Yoder, *Original Revolution*, 13–33. See also Wright, *New Testament and the People of God*, 167–214.

5

The Paradigm Is a Parable

ONE OF THE MOST appropriate texts in the New Testament regarding ethnic and religious division and the hope for reconciliation comes in the form of a parable found only in Luke:

> Then turning to the disciples, Jesus said to them privately, "Blessed are the eyes that see what you see! For I tell you that many prophets and kings desired to see what you see, but did not see it, and to hear what you hear, but did not hear it."
>
> Just then a lawyer stood up to test Jesus. "Teacher," he said, "what must I do to inherit eternal life?" He said to him, "What is written in the law? What do you read there?" He answered, "You shall love the Lord your God with all your heart, and with all your soul, and with all your strength, and with all your mind; and your neighbor as yourself." And he said to him, "You have given the right answer; do this, and you will live."
>
> But wanting to justify himself, he asked Jesus, "And who is my neighbor?" Jesus replied, "A man was going down from Jerusalem to Jericho, and fell into the hands of robbers, who stripped him, beat him, and went away, leaving him half dead. Now by chance a priest was going down that road; and when he saw him, he passed by on the other side. So likewise a Levite, when he came to the place and saw him, passed by on the other side. But a Samaritan

while traveling came near him; and when he saw him, he was moved with pity. He went to him and bandaged his wounds, having poured oil and wine on them. Then he put him on his own animal, brought him to an inn, and took care of him. The next day he took out two denarii, gave them to the innkeeper, and said, 'Take care of him; and when I come back, I will repay you whatever more you spend.' Which of these three, do you think, was a neighbor to the man who fell into the hands of the robbers?" He said, "The one who showed him mercy." Jesus said to him, "Go and do likewise." (Luke 10:23–37 NRSV)

Jesus' primary form of teaching was the parable. The parable is an ancient form of storytelling, considered a subset of the *mashal* (pronounced ma-*shawl*). The parable is akin to a riddle in our society. It was intended to sting; it was to be a sneaky, subversive message in the guise of a story about everyday events and people. Like God showing up in the form of a homeless woman needing to be seen and listened to and loved, Jesus' parables remind us that God comes to us, as he did in a borrowed manger, in unexpected ways. It is important to note that Jesus did not invent parables. For instance, Torah possesses examples of parables, the most famous being the prophet Nathan's stunning parable in the presence of King David in which the prophet names, exposes, and judges the king's secret life. Rather, in his context, Jesus uses parables for his own purposes in describing the essence of the kingdom of God. This is *what* he does and this is *how* he does it.

Here's the story as I read it.

Luke 10:25–37 is perhaps the most important parable Jesus ever offered his first-century hearers. Luke writes that an expert in the law desires to test Jesus. Middle East scholars like Ken Bailey note that the expert is *standing*. In honor and shame cultures, a student sits at the feet of a rabbi as a sign of respect and honor (cf. Luke 10:38–42; Acts 22:3). Even though the would-be student comes to Jesus with an honest question, his motives are not completely pure. By standing, he's essentially testing Jesus with mind, speech, and body. His actions speak louder than his words.[1] Sitting at the feet of a superior is akin to holding the door for a woman; it is a sign of respect. The questioner's standing is a sign that he does not embody in his actions that which he speaks with his lips.

---

1. Bailey, *Poet and Peasant*, 34–35. Bailey devotes all of chapter 3 to this parable (33–56). Much of this is about honor and shame and the first century. There are numerous resources that cover this aspect of life in both Greco-Roman and Jewish culture.

The seemingly hostile inquirer poses a question to Jesus (v. 25): "Teacher, what must I do to inherit eternal life?" To the modern Western mind, the question is about heaven and life after death. However, this is precisely the opposite of what the expert is asking. *Eternal life* is another way of asking about the critical component of Jesus' teaching ministry that the kingdom of God is both present and "on its way." That is, the kingdom is *already* and *not yet.* Jews viewed time in terms of ages, or eons (from the Greek *aeons*)—this age and the age to come. Essentially, the expert is asking something along these lines: "I want to be a part of the world on its way. I want to be a part of God's future in the present. What does *that* look like, Jesus?" The manner in which Jesus handles the expert's question is telling and exposes the Western Christian assumption that the expert wants to know about how to *earn his way to heaven* and the first-century fascination with the age to come.

Because Jesus is a Jew not a Christian, he responds by referring to the pillar of Judaism: love of Torah. He implores the man to remember the heart of their shared faith. Because the expert is a Jew (he is not a Christian either), he responds by quoting Jesus' own teaching, what some theologians have called "Jesus' creed" or "the Jesus Creed"—the essence of Judaism is this: love God with all you have (Deut 6:5) and love your neighbor as much as you love yourself (Lev 19:18). The Jesus Creed stands out to many theologians and New Testament scholars because Jesus takes a popular text (Deut 6:5) and marries it to a relatively obscure text (who reads Leviticus, after all?), then claims that these two texts together provide the center of all of orthodox faith. What we recognize as a brilliant move two thousand years later was borderline heresy and even blasphemy to religious leaders in Israel.

The guy interrogating Jesus has clearly done his homework.

Jesus replies, "Great answer. This is what it really means to be alive." It is important to note that Jesus does not say, "Do this and you will have *eternal life.*" He simply says, "Do you this and you will *live.*" When tested, the student gives the right answer. The story should end here. Everyone should go home feeling like a winner. But it doesn't end here. Luke writes, "But he [the expert] wanted to justify himself"—and so he poses another question to Jesus. Sometimes the questions we ask say more about us than the person we're in conversation with or the answer we receive.

The expert wants to know how to interpret Lev 19:18—after all, there are not many rabbis like Jesus walking around and saying that loving people is *as important as* loving God.[2] The expert wants to know "Who is my neighbor?" which is code for asking, "Who is not my neighbor?" Once you know whom you have to love, you also know whom you do not have to love. Jesus sees this coming a mile away.

Because Jesus is a Jew, he does something typical of Jewish rabbis of his day. He offers a story. Jesus employs the most subversive form of persuasion in the known world: the art of a sneaky story.

A Jew travels south from Jerusalem, the site of the temple, to his home in Jericho. It turns out that Jerusalem is, geographically speaking, *a city on a hill*. The Jewish man is traveling downhill: Jerusalem is twenty-five hundred feet above sea level, while Jericho is eight hundred feet above sea level. While traveling the treacherous road, the man gets attacked—mugged—and is left to die on the side of the road like an animal. Lying naked, he does not have the energy to help himself.

A priest travels down this same road and looks at the man. Upon looking at the man, he passes by on the other side of the road. So too, a Levite comes to the exact same spot as the priest and does the exact same thing: he looks at the man and passes by on the other side.[3] But a Samaritan, unlike the two respected religious leaders, looks at the man, sees his plight, is moved in his spirit, and has immense compassion. The Samaritan does not simply look at the man; he looks *and* he sees him. The compassionate traveler cares for his wounds with the resources he has available. He places the Jew on his own animal, risking being seen as a Samaritan who has beaten up a Jew, and takes the half-dead stranger to a hotel where he pays for all of the man's expenses.

This parable might be best understood in the following fashion: Suppose a Native American finds a cowboy lying in a ditch. The cowboy's been beaten badly. The Native American places the stranger on his horse and rides into Dodge City. After checking into a room over the saloon, the man spends the night taking care of the cowboy. How would the people of Dodge City react to the Native American the following morning when he emerged from the saloon? Most Americans know that they would probably

2. Rabbi Akiva (ca. 50–ca. 135 CE), an important rabbinic figure in ancient literature, also believed that love of neighbor was extremely important. Rabbi Akiva is one of the most mentioned sages in the Mishnah. Thanks to Dr. Amy-Jill Levine for this insight.

3. Amy-Jill Levine notes that many commentators "fail to find the behavior of the priest and the Levite surprising. . . . It is just as likely that Jesus' Jewish listeners would have expected the priest and the Levite to behave compassionately toward the man in the ditch" (*Misunderstood Jew*, 146).

kill him even though he had helped a cowboy. What begins, in Luke 10, as a polite conversation is now an awkward, politically incorrect, one-sided prophetic subversion of ethics, morality, and vision.

Jesus now asks the questions.

I love this. I'm laughing as I type this. Jesus uses a sneaky story to mesmerize the audience, not to mention the *former* expert. "Which of the three men in the story acted as a neighbor to the Jew who got beat up?" asks the rabbi. Jesus' inquisitor, knowing the answer but reluctant to let the word *Samaritan* come from his lips, can only muster a rather lackluster response: "The one who had mercy on him." He can't even allow himself to insinuate that a Samaritan is the hero—a vital clue for our interpretive endeavor. The man's silence is louder than anything he could possibly say.

Jesus ends this exchange by offering a simple exhortation to the lawyer: "Go and be like the Samaritan I just described." Because, for Jesus, the man's question ("Who's my neighbor?") is a bad question built on a faulty premise. The answer to the bad question, in the form of Jesus' sneaky story, is this: *There is no one who is not your neighbor. Everyone is a neighbor. You belong to everyone and everyone belongs to you.* We are all caught up in an inescapable mutuality.[4]

Evangelical Christians are quick to articulate the particularities of why Jesus died (substitutionary atonement) but often slow to understand what got Jesus killed in the first place. Stories like this one—challenging all that is sacred—got Jesus killed. My oldest son, Lucas, is five. Every Easter for the last three years he has asked me, "Why did they kill Jesus?" He never asks me, "Why did Jesus have to die?" He wants to know what got Jesus killed. See the difference?

There's so much going on in this text.

This paradigmatic text is like an onion. The more one peels, the more layers are revealed. There are at least four major layers for American Christians to consider. My assumption here is that this text is a prophetic text intended for Christians regarding our view of Islam globally, and our Muslim neighbors living in the U.S.[5]

---

4. Simon Kistemaker notes that Jesus' questioner is fundamentally a theologian. Jesus understands this and attempts (successfully) to beat him at his own game. Kistemaker, *Parables*, 141.

5. See these scholars for many different takes on the layers of the story: Levine, *Misunderstood Jew*, 144–49; Bailey, *Poet and Peasant*, 33–56; Johnson, *Gospel of Luke*, 171–76 ; Green, *Gospel of Luke*, 424–32; Baker, *Parables*, 140–47.

The first layer is the *do good layer*. In this layer, the most popular interpretation of the ancient parable, the meaning of the parable is straightforward: it is always to *do right by people.* It is always right to choose to help someone, even if it involves a disruption to one's schedule, plans, and daily customs. Therefore, if you have a chance to help a Muslim (or a Buddhist, a Baha'i, even an atheist), you are furthering humanity by aiding, loving, caring, and serving that other person, because our differences pale in comparison to our commonalities. President George W. Bush referenced this understanding of the parable in his first inaugural address: "I can pledge our nation to a goal: When we see that wounded traveler on the road to Jericho, we will not pass to the other side."[6] Likewise, President Obama employed the same rhetoric and understanding of the parable when he honored thirteen U.S. citizens with the Presidential Citizens Medal in October 2011 because "they stopped to help"—echoing Luke 10.[7] In popular culture today, this is the common interpretation of the parable. Newscasts regularly run Good Samaritan stories that usually involve one person helping another on the side of the road or interstate highway. Interestingly, it is also the prevailing interpretive understanding of most lay Christians. I've taught this parable numerous times in churches and universities and have come to this basic conclusion. We have a shallow understanding of what Jesus actually meant when he uttered this subversive story. Shallow isn't getting it done.

I have a friend who teaches philosophy and ethics for a respected liberal arts university. He says that America does not need an ethic of modern-day *Good* Samaritans. Rather, we need a *minimally decent* Samaritan ethic.

My friend is right.

The second layer of interpretation common in the United States (particularly in evangelical circles) is primarily interested in the relationship of purity and love in first-century Judaism and the manner in which Jesus insists on love's superiority to purity. It's just true enough to be convincing but it is far from Jesus' central aim. The second layer highlights the *alleged* tension between the obligation of the two religious leaders and the plight of the forgotten Jewish man left for dead. Levitical code does not allow for the two holy men to tend to the man. While Dr. Amy-Jill Levine, noted New Testament scholar, does not adhere to this understanding, she summarizes

6. George W. Bush, First Inaugural Address, January 20, 2001; see http://www.bartleby.com/124/pres66.html.

7. Tate, "Obama Honors Citizens 'Who Stopped to Help.'"

the second layer well: Were the priests and religious men to care for the man as the Samaritan did, they would become ritually unclean, compromising themselves and their role in the priestly system.[8] Levine categorically rejects this interpretation, and rightfully so. She deconstructs the two main texts from Torah used to support the "unclean" argument (Lev 21:3; Num 19:11). The primary issue with applying these texts is that the man lying in the road isn't dead. Something else is going on:

> The appeal to purity laws for understanding the parable—an appeal the parable never mentions and Luke's Gospel never addresses—actually masks the narrative's surprising implications. All commentators agree that the Samaritan's compassion is a surprise. But they fail to find the behavior of the priest and the Levite surprising as well. It is just as likely that Jesus' Jewish listeners would have expected the priest and the Levite to behave compassionately toward the man in the ditch. Insiders who are *expected* to provide aid do not; outsiders who are not *expected* to show compassion do.[9]

Thus, in this view, which I admit is appealing, Jesus is breaking down the old system of religion and replacing it with a new movement based on love, sacrifice, and reconciliation. Jesus is, after all, the great Jewish reformer in this epistemological approach. He teaches his disciples to choose people over precepts, love over law, responsibility over ritual, and compassion over purity.

Purity and love offer a binary category and can function in an important manner in as much as they are intentionally subverted. There are enough texts in the Gospels to support this second mode of interpretation. However, this approach, as we've proved, does not hold up under reasonable textual and historical scrutiny.

The third layer of interpretation is where things get really interesting, for it is centrally consumed with justice. This layer receives a great deal of attention, and with good reason: its proponents include Dr. King and Cornel West. A fairly recent interpretation, it is what I call the *justice layer*. That is, justice is simply love made public. Love puts on skin and we call it justice. Love becomes public, communal. Fear and power get exposed for the evil twins they continue to be in the human experience.

8. Levine, *Misunderstood Jew*, 145ff.

9. Ibid., 146

In this next interpretive move, the man in the ditch becomes the immigrant profiled by local authorities, the gay couple whom Christians love to hate, the Muslim Americans whom others too quickly stereotype as terrorists, the homeless man urban business owners treat poorly. Luke 10 becomes a rallying cry, which echoes the prophet's charge to God's people to "do justice, love mercy, and walk humbly with God" (Mic 6:8). The most significant textual evidence for this third approach is found in Lev 19:34—a reiteration of 19:18, but with a twist: Israel is to love the other, the *resident alien* among them.

It's a powerful appeal, but it might not quite be what Jesus is doing in the story.[10]

Evangelical and mainline Protestant Christians would do well to follow the logical trajectory of interpretations: from *do good* to *purity* and *love*, to *justice*, to the next category as a way of understanding how this biblical text (and all others) operates as a living word from generation to generation, culture to culture, person to person, situation to situation. Biblical texts do not simply have one meaning. This does not imply that biblical texts can mean anything, but it understands the elastic nature of Torah and the New Testament. Perhaps Dr. King offered the most creative interpretation of the parable in a sermon he preached at New York's Riverside Church during the height of the civil rights movement:

> On the one hand we are called to play the good Samaritan on life's roadside; but that will be only an initial act. One day we must come to see that *the whole Jericho road must be transformed* so that men and women will not be constantly beaten and robbed as they make their journey on life's highway. True compassion is more than flinging a coin to a beggar; it is not haphazard and superficial. It comes to see that an edifice which produces beggars needs restructuring.[11]

---

10. Again, Dr. Levine is insightful: "But as appealing as the message is, it is not quite what the parable conveys, for there is no reason for the majority (or privileged) group to think that the gay man or the homeless woman or the illegal immigrant would harbor hatred against them. To recover the punch of the parable, readers need to see the Samaritans and the Jews as mutually antagonistic" (*Misunderstood Jew*, 148). Mutual antagonism that rivals the mutual suspicion that exists between Christians and Jews, Americans and Middle Easterners.

11. King, "A Time to Break Silence," delivered April 4, 1967; quoted in Washington, *I Have a Dream*, 148. My italics.

The last layer, rarely grasped or taught, is about imagination; it's about getting in the ditch of this story to really grasp Jesus' deeper meaning. Scholars Amy-Jill Levine, Joel Green, and Miroslav Volf make the strongest case for this layer. This deepest layer, the explosive layer in interpreting the oft-domesticated parable, deals with the order of succession of the characters mentioned. It is without a doubt the most literal and literary meaning of the parable, as it rests on the best wisdom we have from history and context. Priests and Levites were significant in Jewish culture, Joel Green writes, though "not because they trained or were chosen to be priests but because they were born into priestly families. They participated and were legitimated by the world of the temple, with its circumspect boundaries between clean and unclean, including clean and unclean people."[12] Essentially, Jesus' audience heard a predictable formula unfolding. Three classes of men staffed the Jerusalem temple: priests, Levites, and laymen. Instead of including another Jewish *character* in the parable—which, if you are counting, would make the *fourth* character in the story Jewish—Jesus surprises his listeners by making the third observer of the man in the ditch a Samaritan. Jesus should have told a story about a Good Jew who helps a lowly Samaritan (interpretive option #1). Instead, he places a volatile character in the middle of this most important exchange. While there is much scholarly debate regarding the manner in which a first-century Jew would have seen a Samaritan, there can be no doubt that a long, bloody history positioned Jews and Samaritans as bitter ethnic and religious rivals. Jews and Samaritans had as much affinity for each other as Northerners and Southerners in America in 1862, Jews and Germans in western Europe in 1940, Hutus and Tutsis in Rwanda at the end of the twentieth century.[13] Once again, Dr. Levine helps us appreciate the text in its historical-literary brilliance:

12. Green, *Gospel of Luke*, 431. It is no small coincidence that, in Luke 9:51–55, Jesus refuses to give in to the request of two disciples' (James and John) to murder (or "nuke") hardened Samaritans. According to Luke, Jesus rebukes them because he understands that ethical tension blinds us to seeing "our enemies" as God sees them, according to the kingdom cadence of Jesus—a truth that he will expound upon in the parable of the Merciful Samaritan.

13. The Tanakh/Old Testament has three critical stories concerning Israel and Samaria's hatred and animosity: Gen 34 (the rape of Dinah), Judg 8 (Abimelech), and 2 Chron 28:8–15 (war and violence). It is also important to note that Jesus sends the disciples, in the beginning of Acts, to Judea *and* Samaria, not Judea *or* Samaria. Because if you've been in one region you don't go to the other. Judeans and Samaritans genuinely disdained each other. It's possible that Judean converts were traveling with the apostles to Samaria.

To understand this parable in theological terms, we need to see the image of God in everyone, not just members of our own group. To hear this parable in contemporary terms, we should think of ourselves as the person in the ditch and then ask, "Is there anyone, from any group, about whom we'd rather die than acknowledge, *She offered help* or *He showed compassion?*" More, is there any group whose members might rather die than help us? If so, then we find the modern equivalent for the Samaritan.

To recognize the shock and the possibility of the parable in practical, political, and pastoral terms, we might translate its first-century geographical and religious concerns into our modern idiom. The ancient kingdom of Samaria is, today, the West Bank. Thus, translated across the centuries, the parable retains the same meaning. The man in the ditch is an Israeli Jew; a rabbi and a Jewish member of the Israeli Knesset fail to help the wounded man, but a member of Hamas shows him compassion.[14]

In North America, the parable might sound something like this. The ancient kingdom is Toronto or Nashville or Dallas or Atlanta—hubs of evangelical Christianity. The man in the ditch is a white Christian; a high-ranking bishop and a prominent Christian leader walk by without having compassion or takin action. A young Muslim, with ties to al-Qaeda, passes by and is moved to action at the sight of one hurting, abandoned. He rescues the suffering man. Both are forever changed.

The parable of the Merciful Samaritan claims that Jesus' disciples need to see the potential for all to act like neighbors: neo-Nazis, the Klan Grand Dragon, as well as the person whose politics differ from one's own.

Theologically, this paradigmatic text is not about belief or action. It is primarily about sight and vision. *How do you see?* The question of seeing/sight is important for, according to this parable, looking and seeing are not the same thing. It's easier to look than it is to see. Immediately preceding this text, Jesus forbids James and John from dropping a nuke on Samaritans, and later says, "Blessed are the eyes that see what you see. For I tell you that many prophets and kings wanted to see what you see but did not see it" (10:23–24).

Furthermore, the word for being moved with compassion or pity (*splagchnizomai*) in 10:33 is the same word that appears in the parable of the two sons in Luke 15, in which the father sees his lost son running toward

---

14. Levine, *Misunderstood Jew*, 148–49. The film *Crash* (Lions Gate, 2004) captured the hearts and minds of many in the Western world. The ending, which I will not delve into at this point, is probably the perfect embodiment of this fourth interpretive option.

him and is filled with compassion (15:20). *Splagchnizomai*, a fairly uncommon word in the New Testament, is the strongest word for compassion in the Greek language. Literally, it means "to be moved in one's bowels."

Paul offers a similar teaching in his letter to urban Christians trying to overcome racial and religious differences in light of Jesus' resurrection: "So from now on, we regard no one from a worldly point of view. . . . The old has gone, the new is here" (2 Cor 5:16–17).

Having compassion, pity, and regard are about one thing: seeing. Recently many writers and theologians have written about the need for Christians, and people of all faiths, to develop *double vision*. That is, when it comes to friends, strangers, and enemies, Jesus invites Christians not to simply *look*, but to further cultivate the art of *seeing*. Two thousand years ago, Jesus implored his disciples to look and see; Jesus' message to his disciples in twenty-first-century America is no different.

Christians can stand from within a particular story while also appreciating other stories. We can be followers of Jesus while also appreciating those who follow other traditions. In *Exclusion and Embrace*, Croatian theologian Miroslav Volf unpacks these concepts. In the context of the Croatian-Serbian conflict of the 1990s, Volf discusses forgiveness as the only thing that will stop the journey from exclusion to abuse. He describes double vision as an important part of forgiveness, peace, and reconciliation. Double vision is about "letting the voices and perspectives of others, especially those with whom we may be in conflict, resonate within ourselves, by allowing them to help us see them, as well as ourselves, from *their* perspective, and if needed, readjust our perspectives as we take into account their perspectives."[15] Lee Camp, ethicist and recent writer on the subject of Muslims and Christian in dialogue internationally, adds to Volf's work by noting that double vision is a call to intellectual humility: "We are all finite human beings, belabored not only with our finitude but also with our prejudices and presuppositions and our own experiences."[16]

Action and vision are mutual; they go together. Sometimes action compels one to see differently. Sometimes seeing differently causes one to act in new ways. The paradigmatic parable at hand is direct: the praxis component of Jesus' answer to the expert was to not just redefine neighbor

15. Volf, *Exclusion and Embrace*, 213. Volf also writes, "Double vision . . . is the epistemological side of faith in the crucified" (214). See John 9 for an excellent biblical example of double vision.

16. Camp *Who Is My Enemy?*, 6. Camp offers a remarkable treatment of the entire subject of "seeing" at 6–12.

or not let him turn it into "who is not my neighbor?" Rather, the point is to completely reframe the whole issue so that *any* answers to who is or who is not my neighbor become irrelevant. The definition of one's neighbor (the theoretical issue) is completely taken over in the story by the praxis charge: *Be a neighbor*—no more questions or answers required. This is Jesus at his prophetic best.

6

The Bible Jesus Read

Neither beasts nor angels, we live in twilight, and we are unsure
whether it is a prelude to morning or night.

—Andrew Sullivan

As I BEGAN RESEARCHING the theological vision of the New Testament
regarding Jews and Samaritans (and, ultimately, Christians and Muslims),
I felt a nagging question repeatedly surface—a question that relentlessly
pursued me in the three years I spent reading, researching, interviewing,
and discussing the relationship between Jews and Samaritans, Christians
and Muslims.

Questions are often more important than answers. If one asks poor
questions, the answers are doomed from the beginning. As the questions
improve, the answers improve.

How did Jesus arrive at the brilliant, liberating, life-altering theology
of Luke 10? I want Jesus to show his homework. What were his sources?
I've thought about this question a great deal. Did he know because, after all,
he had an inside connection to Torah's divine meaning for Jews in the first
century? Did he receive direct revelation via visions and dreams, thus making him the supernatural teacher of his day? Or is there perhaps something
else going on in Jesus' imagination and primary view of God and God's
world?

THE BIBLE JESUS READ

I want to know why Jesus was so freaking brilliant.

Here's the answer that I have discovered. At least the answer I'm going with right now.

The first book of the Bible is the key. It turns out that the Old Testament (or Hebrew Scriptures) counts more than Christians are willing to admit. I can't prove it, but I think Mary, Joseph, and his immediate context immersed Jesus in the sacred pages of Torah to such a degree that he began to see the world primarily through the lens (questions, values, assumptions, etc.) of Genesis.

Genesis—in case you have not considered it before—is a theological drama that gives humanity our place in the present and future through the pathway of the past. Genesis prods our imaginations to remember the God (*elohim*) who creates (*bara*) out of nothing and chaos. Through God's spoken word, light and darkness are separated. Sky and water torn apart. And what God separates, God fills with sun, moon, stars, animals, birds, fish, and vast oceans. God calls all of this good.

The material world is intended for our pleasure. Oceans. Books. Ice cream. Baseball. Chocolate. Good movies. Homemade cookies. A perfect sunset.

You get the picture.

The Genesis creation account comes to a dramatic climax near the end of chapter 1. Just as the gospels build toward the resurrection of Jesus, Genesis builds toward the grand entrance of humans on center stage of the cosmic drama that has been unfolding in the previous twenty-plus verses.

Before Islam and Christianity were at war . . .

Before the Holocaust . . .

Before religious tribalism and denominational competition . . .

Before atomic weaponry . . .

Before Hiroshima and Nagasaki . . .

Before the American slave trade or modern-day sex trafficking . . .

An ancient book that still captures the head and the heart.

Consider three texts that describe the infusion of humans into the divine drama.

Genesis 1:26: In this story, the angelic hosts are a witness to God's creation of *adam* (humankind). In this section, the text is very clear that both male and female equally reflect God. That is, the picture is not one of hierarchy but of equality. God is not a gendered being; men and women are. Women equally reflect the nature and character of God. God does not have a penis.

Genesis 2:7: The first human is formed from the dust of the ground and possesses the spirit of God, because God has breathed into *adam* animate life, just as God's spirit brought life out of the chaos in Gen 1:1–2.

Genesis 2:18: God sees that the first human is alone. God sends Adam into a deep sleep, then uses Adam's rib to fashion a partner for him. The word is literally "helper" (*ezer*, pronounced *ay-zer*)—a word most often used to describe God in the Hebrew Scriptures. Whereas woman's ability to reproduce in chapter 1 is a pragmatic description of one of her gifts to creation, here the reader is introduced to the emotional completeness that can be experienced in the context of this relationship: sexual, emotional, and spiritual intimacy so profound that Adam breaks into the first country song ever recorded (Gen 2:23 is classical music): *I'm so lonely, I could cry. Now the good Lord has given me someone to love, I can't believe my eyes.*

Humans take center stage in these accounts. We are the only element of creation that causes God not to say "good" but "very good." God is most pleased with what God has done by forming man and woman. The word *image*, which in Hebrew is *selem*, is usually understood in terms of essential characteristics. That is, humans are like God in that we love, care, feel, have authority, exercise justice. And there's more going on in these texts than we acknowledge. It's probably better to translate *selem* as *icon*. The word *humankind* should probably be translated "The Adam" since it refers, in chapter 1, to both male and female, or specifically, a nongendered universal human. Thus, we might understand the power of Genesis 1 if we read the text in this way: God creates The Adam. God splits the lonely The Adam into *Ish* (man) and *Ishah* (woman). God then brings *Ish* (man) and *Ishah* (woman) back together again as one complete flesh. Because just as God is complete in community, so too are humans. Scholars like Walter Brueggemann, Sarah Coakley, and Scot McKnight describe some version of the following:

God creates . . .

The Adam,

then splits the lone *The Adam* into . . .

Ish in communion with *Ishah,*

who are brought together by God to form . . .

One flesh.

Mr. and Mrs. *Icon* bear God's image to the rest of the world in mysterious ways. In ancient Near Eastern creation narratives, *icon* was royal or kingship language. In the ancient Near East it was widely believed that a god's spirit lived in any statue or image of that god, with the result that the image could function as a kind of representative of or substitute for the god wherever it was placed. In this time and place, the king often "stood in the place of" the gods. Therefore, Genesis is saying that humans exercise dominion and authority over creation simply because they are human. There is not one king but many kings who have a high calling to live in shalom with the rest of creation.

Kingship gets democratized. I'm suggesting that, it its context, Genesis was revolutionary. As revolutionary as "Letter from a Birmingham Jail" was in the 1960s, as revolutionary as the Declaration of Independence was at the close of the eighteenth century, and as revolutionary as the Magna Carta or the ideas of Plato.

One can't possibly underestimate how radical this is in light of other creation stories embedded within ancient Mesopotamian culture. Every person who inhabits earth bears the stamp of royalty. Regardless of race, ethnicity, or religion—Genesis declares that God's image is stamped upon every person. The psalmist agrees: "When I behold your heavens, the work of your fingers, the moon and stars that you set in place, what is man that you have been mindful of him, mortal man that you have taken note of him, that you have made him little less than divine, and adorned him with glory and majesty; you have made him your master over your handiwork" (Ps 8:3–6).[1]

A few years ago, I visited Cowboys Stadium in Arlington, Texas, appropriately nicknamed "Jerry's World" after the owner of the NFL's Dallas Cowboys, Jerry Jones. Built for $1.4 billion dollars, the super-sized stadium is already being called the Eighth Wonder of the World. The original

---

1. Scot McKnight told me recently in conversation that he believes that there are four "enemies" in American life: 1) Muslims, 2) gay and lesbian persons, 3) those whose politics differ from mine, and 4) the poor. We have to get serious about applying this teaching from Genesis to these four areas. We could call this the theological equivalent of *Guess Who's Coming to Dinner?*

Cowboys Stadium, built in the 1970s, cost less ($37 million) than the jumbo replay screens ($40 million) hanging from the ceiling in the new stadium.

Aside from the decent spiral touchdown pass I threw to my friend Dean in the end zone during our visit, I was most impressed by the contrast between the man who occupies the owner's suite, Jerry's Perch, during Cowboys home games and Rosa, the Hispanic woman cleaning the bathrooms as I toured the locker room. Genesis, at the beginning of the sacred Torah, claims that both billionaire and janitor equally reflect God's light and glory in the world.

This isn't simply a Jewish or Christian idea worth supporting. This is good for all humans. Phillip Yancey captures this teaching in Genesis when he writes, "How can we admire Miss Universe without devaluing the fifteen-year-old high school girl who wears glasses, has pimples, and whose figure resembles a lamppost? Or how can we honor Bill Gates and also the man who empties Bill Gates's garbage?"[2]

Several years ago, a rabbi and scholar of Jewish teaching taught me that the name of God (which Jews do not pronounce) actually forms the human body. If we place the name of God—which, in its purest form, has only four letters—from top to bottom and trace those letters from head to toe, we realize that Genesis' claim that humans bear the image of God is not simply an esoteric, intellectualized way to get people to behave well. Rather, this truth is embedded in every person we encounter.

Put down this book and practice writing the name of God on someone (preferably someone you know). The first letter forms the face. The second forms the shoulders and arms. The third forms the core/middle of the body, and the fourth letter, same in structure as the second, forms the waist and legs.

Seriously, you need to do this experiment. You will thank me.

---

2. Yancey, *What Good Is God?*, 107–8.

If you are reading this and still haven't tried it, put the book down and trace the four letters of God's sacred name on the person nearest you, then tell them, "You bear the name of God on your body."

First letter forms the face. Second letter forms the shoulders and arms. Third letter forms the core of the body. Fourth letter (same as the second) forms the waist and legs.

Yes, this is a full-contact reading experience!

If they look at you funny, blame it on me. If they open up to you, blame it on God.

How would coming to see the truth of this name on our bodies change the way we think about the vitriolic e-mails we forward in the name of humor or the off-color jokes we tell in the privacy of people just like us? How would it affect the way we engage in debates about health care for the poor or hospitality for those who are not yet citizens? (Whether you lean left or right, it should change the tenor of the conversation.)

How would it radically alter the way we view our Muslim neighbors?

Understanding the image-of-God-truth embedded in every person is what prompted Jesus to say that the entirety of his mission could be summed up in loving God and loving others—and it is why Jesus taught us to pray for those who would do us harm: those who persecute us, our enemies.

Jesus' brother, no doubt influenced by this core principle, wrote, "With the tongue we praise our Lord and Father, and with it we curse people who have been made in God's likeness" (Jas 3:9). All of these teachings were rooted in the Leviticus witness that loving the neighbor and the alien was the very essence of keeping all of the other commandments.

Because I'm a Christian (and a minister/theologian *within* the Christian tradition), my primary orientation to the world is the life and teachings of Jesus. If, however, my Christianity does not exhibit the radical, inclusive love of others (which Jesus taught and personified), then my Christianity becomes something it was never intended to be. The teachings of both the Jewish and Christian Scriptures call us into the deep waters of an ancient spirituality that—despite hypocrisy, murder, war, and strife—still stands as a remarkable vision for human life on Earth. These teachings can help us overcome vitriolic diatribes on the left or the right and the demonization of one religious group by another.

It seems that two options, both of them bad, have emerged in North America regarding interaction between Christians and Muslims. Option 1: Passionate and hostile (common in fundamentalist and evangelical Americans). Option 2: Laissez-faire and indifferent (common in liberal and post-Christian Americans).

It's time for a third way: Passionate and engaged. Fervent and open. Unapologetically Christian to such a degree that I'm not threatened, afraid, or scared of someone else's faith, *even if that faith is supposed to be my rival and enemy.*

This third way is based upon Jesus' clear and direct teaching in Luke 10, which is based upon the clear and direct teaching in Genesis 1 and 2.

The third way emerges as we take Genesis more seriously. It does not instantly light up with anger, nor does it grow indifferent and absent. A third way demands more than the other ways and also offers the greatest potential for understanding and true relationship.

Genesis makes it clear that we all (seven billion strong) bear the divine image of the one God who made this world and everything in it. The burden of bearing the divine image is this: we must all learn to see this not only in ourselves and the ones we feel comfortable with. We must also learn to see this divine spark in every person who crosses our path.

This is the foundation upon which the parable of the Merciful Samaritan is built. This is central to the Jesus Story.

The Icon Human

This is what I'm suggesting: Genesis makes the bold claim that humans are the paradoxical and perfect intersection of spirit and body; God and creation kiss in the form of humanity—divinity and dust. C. S. Lewis aptly describes this paradox: "Humans are amphibians—half spirit and half animal. . . . As spirits they belong to the eternal world, but as animals they inhabit time. This means while their spirit can be directed to an eternal object, their bodies, passions, and imaginations are in continual change, for to be in time means to change. Their nearest approach to constancy, therefore, is undulation."[3]

Judaism, Christianity, and Islam basically agree upon the sacred nature of the body in light of the one Creator, God. For Judaism in the first century (as well as for orthodox Christianity and Islam today), heaven was not a physical location related to eternity. Heaven is the *realm of God* where all is well and things are as they should be. Hell, then, is its opposite. Hell is not the furthest south one can go; it's the space and realm where all is dark, evil—opposing love, mercy, and hope.

That's why Jesus says you'd better address the animal in you or the delusional angel you've created now, or else you will find yourself completely consumed in the things of darkness.

When we wake up in the morning and look around us, wondering who we are, where we are, how we got here, where we came from, how we fit into what's going on, the answer is the same: *In the beginning . . . God created . . .*

Whether it's religious abuse, racism, exploitation, or sex, Christians are called to live in the midst of a world that is full of light and dark, flesh and spirit, divinity and humanity.

Earth is crammed with heaven and mud.

So we enter into relationship with people who are "other" than us because we believe that beyond their humanity, or in the midst of their humanity, we also see the divine, eternal imprint of God.

I love the way the following story illustrates the truth of every human being bearing the divine image of God:

> Several years ago one of my students who lived a distance away
> and rode a crowded bus to the college each day said to his wife as
> he went out the door one morning, "I'm just going to go out and

3. Lewis, *Screwtape Letters*, 40.

immerse myself in God's creation today." The next day his parting words were the same. On the third day, she called him back,
"Don't you think you ought to go to class today? A couple of days
of walking in the woods or on the beach is okay, but don't you
think enough is enough?"

He said, "Oh, I've been going to class every day."

"Then what," she said, "is all this business about immersing
yourself in creation?"

"Well, I spend forty minutes on the bus each morning and
afternoon. Can you think of a setting more thick with creation
than that—all these people *created*, created in the image of God,
created male and female?"

"I never thought of that," she said.

"You mean you've never read Genesis?"[4]

Imagine that a rabbi, imam, and Christian minister walk into a bar . . . and
the bartender says, "Did you know you were created in the image of God?"

The rabbi says, "Of course, it's in Genesis."

The imam says, "I've heard something along those lines."

The minister says, "You mean Christians are not the only ones created
in the image of God?"

The rabbi and imam look at each other, then at the minister and say,
"Seriously?"

"I'll have to think about this and get back to you," stammers the
minister.

Lipstick (Divine) Love

In 1945, Lieutenant Colonel M. W. Gonin led a group of British soldiers in
liberating a large concentration camp. In his journal, he gives an account of
the dehumanization they encountered:

I can give no adequate description of the Horror Camp in which
my men and myself were to spend the next month of our lives. It
was just a barren wilderness, as bare as a chicken run. Corpses lay
everywhere, some in huge piles, sometimes they lay singly or in
pairs where they had fallen.

It took a little time to get used to seeing men, women and
children collapse as you walked by them. . . . One knew that
five hundred a day were dying and that five hundred a day were

4. This story is told by Eugene Peterson in *Christ Plays in Ten Thousand Places*, 82.

going to go on dying before anything we could do would have the slightest effect. It was, however, not easy to watch a child choking to death from diphtheria when you knew a tracheotomy and nursing would save it. One saw women drowning in their own vomit because they were too weak to turn over and men eating worms as they clutched half a loaf of bread purely because they had to eat and could now scarcely tell the difference between worms and bread. Piles of corpses, naked and obscene, with a woman too weak to stand propping herself up against them as she cooked the food we had given her over an open fire; men and women crouching down just anywhere in the open relieving themselves . . . a woman standing stark naked washing herself with some issue soap in water from a tank in which the remains of a child floated.[5]

The troops cared for the victims of genocide in ways that go beyond description. One by one. Wounds bandaged, tears wiped, stitches sewed, broken limbs set in casts. These soldiers demonstrated in a powerful way what it means to look at the world and fellow humans with *new creation* eyes.[6]

It was shortly after the British Red Cross arrived, though it may have no connection, that a very large quantity of lipstick arrived. This was not at all what we wanted, we were screaming for hundreds and thousands of other things and I don't know who asked for lipstick.

I wish so much that I could discover who did it. It was the action of genius, sheer unadulterated brilliance. I believe nothing did more for these internees than the lipstick. Women lay in bed with no sheets and no nightie but with scarlet red lips, you saw them wandering about with nothing but a blanket over their shoulders, but with scarlet red lips. I saw a woman dead on the postmortem table and clutched in her hand was a piece of lipstick.

At last someone had done something to make them individuals again; they were someone, no longer merely the number tattooed on the arm. At last they could take an interest in their appearance. That lipstick started to give them back their humanity.

They weren't animals. They weren't angels.
They were women created in God's image.

---

5. Lieutenant Colonel Gonin's account has been published in numerous books, and (in part) online; my primary source for this extract and the one that follows is Bell, *Sex God*, 18 and 30, but see also Reilly, *Belsen in History and Memory*, 136–37.

6. Quoted in an exhibit by graffiti artist Banksy, Imperial War Museum (Banksy, *Wall and Piece*).

Thank God someone remembered.

And so it is with Samaritans, according to Jesus. It isn't first about politics or religion or tribe . . . but first, humanity.

And so it is with our Muslim neighbors. This is the heart of Judaism and Christianity. It is the literal reading and meaning of the core of the parable of the Merciful Samaritan.

The *Enuma Elish* and *Epic of Gilgamesh* were two popular ancient creation myths rivaling the Genesis narrative in the ancient world. Each depicts humans as nothing more than pawns or side notes. Not so in the Genesis story. For in this story, *The Story of Us*, humans take center stage and learn to play our role, not as animals or angels (the universe has enough of those) but as humans, God's intended extension in the world. Irenaeus reminds us that the *glory of God is a person fully alive*. Are you living? Are you playing the role God meant for you to play? Is this the script you are living?

Because sometimes you can't know the true story if you don't first know the false ones. Here's Genesis 1 and 2 (and lipstick love) in living color. This is the foundational material, which funded Jesus' imagination as he learned to put Torah into practice as depicted in parable form in Luke 10.

The recent film *Of Gods and Men* shows us what this kind of radical commitment to the humanity/divinity in every person looks like in the flesh. It's the story of the monks of Tibhirine, a monastery in Algeria; of the community they love; and of militant Muslims who threaten all they know and love.

> For approximately sixty years the monastery had been a Christian presence and a witness to the surrounding Muslim neighbors, with whom the monks enjoyed excellent relations. However, in the early 1990s, the monks found themselves caught up in a violent conflict between the Algerian government and radical Islamic rebels who wished to turn the country into an Islamic state, free of all foreigners. As most foreigners fled the country, the monks decided it was their duty to stay with their Muslim neighbors who were suffering at the hands of the rebels.
>
> On Christmas Eve 1993, the monastery was taken over by an armed group of rebels. The monks knew that the rebels had recently massacred a group of Croatian Catholic construction workers. Courageously, the head of the monastery, aptly named Father Christian, demanded that the rebels leave so that he and

his monks could celebrate the birth of Christ. The rebels left but promised they would be back. For two years, even as reports came in that the rebels had killed other Christians, the monks, against all odds, stayed, prayed, read the Bible, and served and witnessed to their Muslim neighbors. With the prospect of the rebels return-ing at any moment, the spiritual life of the monks took on a new intensity. They had found a new sense of life by living on the edge of death. By offering up their lives and living with the threat of death every day, they had discovered holiness.

Christopher Jamison wrote of the monks, "The origin of *sacri-fice* is the Latin *sacrum facere*—'to make holy.' So as you offer your life on the altar, God blesses you and makes you holy. During those two years the monks offered themselves in communion each day: in return, God blessed them and made them holy." In early 1996 the rebels made good on their promise to return. Father Christian and six other monks were murdered, their throats sliced. They had found their true selves by giving up their lives. . . .

Before his death . . . Father Christian wrote a letter to be opened in case of his death. . . . [He] wrote the following message to the radical Islamic terrorist he was sure would return to kill him: "To you, my last-minute friend, who will not have known what you are doing: yes, I want this thank you and this adieu to be for you, too, because in God's face I see you. May we meet again as thieves in Paradise, if it pleases God, the Father of us both."[7]

". . . the Father of us both . . . the Father of us both . . ." I can't get that phrase out of my mind and out of my heart. These monks were not trying to get their fifteen seconds of fame. They had no desire to capture the interest of Hollywood or Paris. They were indifferent to the world's media machine. They simply chose to be true to a commitment they had already made in their baptism. They were already dead. They were ready for God to do a new thing. That's the hope of the nations—God raising us once we are will-ing to die.

Up to this point, we've kept most of our attention on Luke and Gen-esis. But, of course, Matthew's Gospel contains one of the most dynamic and arresting texts on the challenge of the Jesus Way:

> "You have heard that it was said, 'You shall love your neighbor and hate your enemy.' But I say to you, Love your enemies and pray for those who persecute you, so that you may be children of your Father in heaven; for he makes his sun rise on the evil and on the

7. Sayers, *Vertical Self*, 164–65, 67–68.

good, and sends rain on the righteous and on the unrighteous. For if you love those who love you, what reward do you have? Do not even the tax collectors do the same? And if you greet only your brothers and sisters,what more are you doing than others? Do not even the Gentiles do the same? Be perfect, therefore, as your heavenly Father is perfect." (Matt 5:43–48)

Jesus' direct teaching on ethnic and religious tension should move us to look into the deepest places in our soul and to ask the deeper questions of identity, hatred, reconciliation, and God's future.

"Because the worst day in human history didn't happen on a Tuesday," preaches William Willimon.

Because "I really only love God as much as the person I love the least," claims Dorothy Day.

Because "Jesus would rather go to hell than send his enemies there," writes Greg Boyd.

Here's the question we must hold onto: Did Jesus go to the cross because we couldn't possibly love our enemies, or was it that he thought we could but that we first needed to see it done? The manner in which you answer this question will be the foreshadowing of how you approach the tension and animosity between Muslims and Christians in the U.S. For Jesus people, the cross is the source and shape of salvation, the primary way we move forward, trying to align our life with Jesus' life. The cross is the way God redeemed and restored the world, and it's still the way God redeems and restores the world.

Now we know the heart of the Jesus way. The Bible Jesus read (Torah) prepared him for the world he was trying to live in. That's the function of sacred scripture. If the text doesn't create the space for creative engagement, it's a spiritual miscarriage. Or, in the words of the writer of the Fourth Gospel, *word becomes flesh*. That's how it works in God's theological ecosystem.

Now we know the heart of the Bible Jesus read. Let's go even deeper.

7

Jesus with Skin

IN JESUS' TEACHINGS, HE is clear that in his kingdom *there is no one who is not a neighbor* (Luke 10:25–37). That is, everyone is a neighbor; everyone is invited to be a neighbor to her neighbor. His disciples, despite ample opportunity, are not allowed to have enemies—the assumption being that Jesus' disciples desire to bring the things of heaven to earth.

Because we only love God as much as the person we love the least.

Disciples and Christians are to love others as Christians claim to love God. The Jesus Creed—loving God and others—is built upon the Genesis conviction that every person bears the image of God and that Jesus' disciples are to make prayer and conversation with those deemed *enemies* a part of the spiritual disciplines that mark a community of faith (Matt 5–7).

Jesus physically interacted with a Samaritan (John 4), one marginalized in much the same way we marginalize Muslims today. He had many chances to engage in bitter conflict with the enemies of his people (Israel), and yet he refused to do so (see, e.g., Luke 9:51–56). In short, Jesus exposed the walls constructed by ethnic, sociological, and religious abuse. Jesus then proceeded to tear down the walls that divide and to see others as God sees all of creation (2 Cor 5).[1]

---

1. See also Luke 9:52; 10:33; 17:16; John 4:9, 40; Acts 8:25. Today a few Samaritans

This is the teaching Jesus gives the Christian community today. How this Jesus-truth implicates specific governments—particularly in primarily Christian nations whose politics are influenced by Christianity—is a different and greater discussion for another day. The church's first calling is to be the church made in Jesus' image, the church of God's intent. I'm writing to the church, not the governments of modern nation-states.

Some Christians are afraid of Islam.

Other Christians are indifferent.

Still others are pursuing a third way, a better way.

I hope you agree when I say that the time is now for liberal and evangelical Christians in America to let go of our need for enemies. It is time for us to release the love of hate and the fear of the unknown. It is time to stop looking and start seeing. Why should we continue to define ourselves by who we are not, rather than who we are? Why should we continue to define ourselves by our hatred of enemies instead of by our love for the one who came to end division among ethnic and religious groups?

Combining Genesis' radical teaching about the nature of humanity and the sacredness of God with Jesus' teaching in the parable of the Good Samaritan, local churches can affirm the following principles:

All human life is *equally* valuable.

Because all life comes *from* God.

And because all humans reflect the divine image, even if it is harder to detect in some than in others.

Christianity thus asserts that God became human (the Word became flesh) to show us the *kind of human he intended each one of us to be*, even going so far as to die for us, his enemies. This is the essence of Jesus' gospel, the kingdom of God.

Jesus' resurrection is the ultimate end to all forms of dualism, especially ethnic, religious, and social animosity.

The resurrection is God's vindication of Jesus' identity and strategy of human engagement and actualization. The cross event, then, is not simply the source of creation's salvation; the cross is also the

---

survive, not having lost their identity through intermarriage. There are about three hundred active practitioners of the Samaritan religion, most of whom live in the city of Nablus. Although their temple is long since destroyed, they still celebrate Passover every year in its ruins on Mount Gerazim.

shape of creation's salvation. Death precedes life. A resurrection is only possible if there is first death.

The church does not have a mission; it *is* a mission—reconciling the world from its love of hate, division, walls, and animosity. The church is inherently missional.

This is the kingdom logic. This is the creed we should be teaching our children and grandchildren. I long for the day when Christian churches are known for being on the forefront of understanding, dialogue, interaction, service, and appreciation for our Muslim neighbors out of the conviction that we do not get to decide who is "neighbor" and who is "enemy."

That is, I long for the day when churches implement this creed.

Jesus has already rejected the false premise that people of different faiths cannot love one another and has called us to be a neighbor to every person we encounter. To become a Christian is, essentially, an act of learning the story of Jesus and Israel so well that one can interpret and experience oneself and the world in terms of that story. The task of the Christian church is to know the ancient script so well that we know how to perform the story in our time and place. The Muslim today is the Samaritan of yesterday. The Muslim of Christianity's *now* is the Samaritan of Jesus' *then*.

As much as I love reading (and writing), I sometimes think that reading a book (like the one you are reading right now) can mislead you into thinking that you are in fact *doing something* to address the issue. Of course, you *are* doing something, you *are* reading, but reading is only the beginning. The ideas in this book will remain only mildly dangerous to the status quo unless someone decides to put them into practice.

For me, this entire discussion is not just communal and social, it is deeply personal. To explain what I mean, let me introduce you to Cameron.

My friend Cameron Hunt knows intimately the power of shame, isolation, and hate as it relates to religious identity. Cameron, whose real name is Cameron Hosseini, is from small-town Mississippi, but he was born in Tehran, Iran. His biological father, Seyed Hosseini, was a tall, dark, educated, handsome man. His mother, a U.S. citizen who had given birth to another son (Amir) before Cameron was born, simply wanted to visit her home state of Mississippi to show off her two sons to her biological family in the States. After the mom and two sons visited the U.S., Cameron's father became paranoid and abusive toward his wife. I do not mean to imply that his father was abusive *because* he was Muslim (the majority-Christian U.S.

has one of the highest domestic abuse rates of any modern country). I mention it because I want to bring you into their particular journey.

After months and months of plotting, Cameron's mother took Amir and Cameron back to the U.S. where they lived with family, in great fear of retaliation from their father. They did not run because of shame. They ran because they feared for their lives.

One would hope for a grand ending to what was a difficult beginning to Cameron's life. However, a deep sense of shame overcame Cameron as he grew up in the Mississippi public school system. I interviewed Cameron for this book, and he opened up to me:

> I came to the U.S. when I was two. I did not begin to experience shame until I entered elementary school. My name appeared in the annual yearbook at the conclusion of kindergarten as Cameron Hosseini—the word was out, and I knew they all knew I was not one of them. When I returned to school the next year, many kids began intense name-calling. On the playground I began to experience deep shame as I was inundated with names such as "camel rider" and "sand nigger." I could not understand their venom. I didn't have the tools to process their hate. I was all alone in my hidden shame.
>
> As I grew older (and even after my name was changed to Hunt when my mother remarried), I was still terrified that the other *theys* would find out I was not one of *them*. I was terrified people would associate me with my Middle Eastern name if they found out. I was afraid that a woman would never love me because at some point I would have to come clean. This is why I suppressed the story until I was twenty-six and spiritually bankrupt. It wasn't until I was in graduate school, taking a course about human identity and the role of narrative, that I unleashed the entire story: the good, the bad, the ugly *and the shame*. It wasn't until I released this story that I began to feel the power of Jesus's resurrection at work in my life.

If only Cameron knew, as a little boy, Genesis's radical claim: he bears the image of a King; not because he's Iranian or Muslim or American or Christian, but because he's human.

As a young boy, Cameron was acutely aware of the size of his nose and the fear that he might be *outed* as a Middle Easterner—one of *them*. All of that pain pushed Cameron to hide. His hiding place? The golf course. It became his escape. He eventually became a three-time high school golf champion in the state of Mississippi. Thoughts of hopelessness, despair, and suicide eventually subsided.

Fast forward to Cameron's late twenties, when after years of running he realized that the problem was *within* and that everyplace he went, the shame of his past went with him. It wasn't until he ceased running that he dealt with who he really was before friends and God. Cameron, by the grace of God, was able to lay down the shotgun he pressed into his mouth one morning in Mississippi, and receive the grace and power Jesus was offering. God has no stepchildren or grandchildren—only sons and daughters. The Bible Jesus read prepared him to embody this truth in his divisive culture. Cameron is now passionate about Christian-Muslim engagement because, for him, it is essential; it is woven into the very fabric of his humanity. It's in his DNA.

Islam is small but growing in our context.

Negative stereotypes are dangerous, and they are everywhere.

Immigration changes mean more Muslim neighbors will be moving into neighborhoods and schools.

Jesus—because of his Jewish roots—offers a twenty-first-century answer to a first-century question. The local church has incredible potential to make a difference.

And there's one more element to this that will surprise you.

Here we go.

8

Jesus and Rivalry

He who knows one, knows none.

—Max Müller

THE PARABLE OF THE Merciful Samaritan is quite direct. The point of Jesus' answer to the expert is not just to redefine neighbor, nor is it to let him turn it into "who is not my neighbor?" Rather, the point is to completely reframe the whole issue so that *any* answer to *who is* or *who is not* my neighbor becomes irrelevant. The definition of one's neighbor (the theoretical issue) is completely taken over in the story by Jesus' charge: "Be a neighbor"—no more questions or answers required.

I believe there is no more concrete parallel to the tension between the Samaritan and Jew in New Testament times than the animosity that exists today between Muslims and Christians.[1] What the Samaritan was to the Jew, the Muslim is to the Christian. What the Jew was to the Samaritan, the Christian is to the Muslim.

1. See the bibliography for books comparing and contrasting Islam, Christianity, and Judaism. Regarding Christianity and Islam: Jesus and Muhammad are often pitted against each other. It would probably be better to compare Jesus to the Qur'an (divine revelation); Mary, Jesus' mother, to Muhammad (the ones who bring the Word of God into the world); and the Bible to the hadith. This is an important area for studies in comparative religion. If you are looking for a focus for a master's thesis or doctoral dissertation, there it is.

That's the center, the bottom line, the foundation of this entire book. Write it down. Memorize it. Take a picture.

Jesus intended to do something, as a vital component of the kingdom of God, about the tension between Jews and Samaritans,[2] who held many convictions in common. It would be a mistake to naively suggest that Samaritans and Jews were the same—that they were traveling up the same mountain though taking different paths. But Jews and Samaritans had more commonalities than they had differences. They practiced strict monotheism, being passionate in their belief in and worship of the one God. Both avoided the making of images, for idolatry is forbidden. Both called themselves the children of Israel. They shared the belief that they were the chosen people of God. Each group possessed strong attachment to the land given to their fathers. They also held to the law of Moses, as shown by their observance of the Sabbath, their use of circumcision, and their celebration of festivals. Both believed eschatology was *Mashiach*-centric: hope and conviction that the *Mashia* (messiah) would deliver them (the Samaritans believed in the *Taheb* not the *Christos*). Finally, both clung to an expectation of a glorious destiny—heaven.

To be sure, the two had their differences. But the differences have to be considered in light of their similarities. Here are differences: the Samaritans implemented a different holy book—the Samaritan Pentateuch was considered the only authoritative Scripture and it varied from the Jewish Scriptures. Samaritans also had other texts that were considered authoritative, such as the *Memar Markah*, the Samaritan liturgy and Samaritan law codes. Samaritans developed their own priesthood (Samaritans were not from the tribe of Levi). Samaritans also performed different worship practices and rituals. They faced Mt. Gerazim when they prayed; they mixed aspects of mysticism with elements of true worship in the Jewish Scripture. Samaritans produced different religious teachings and writings, and they thought of the Holy Spirit as the *preexistent Moses* and linked Mt. Gerazim to the garden of Eden where Noah's ark landed, Abraham tried to sacrifice Isaac, and God instructed Israel to build the temple.

And yet, Jesus made one Samaritan a hero (Luke 10) and another Samaritan (a woman no less!) the first evangelist in the kingdom of God (John

2. Evidence of the tension between these two groups is found in John 8:48, in which religious leaders accuse Jesus of being a Samaritan possessed by a demon. This was no compliment. The origin of Samaritans goes back to 2 Kgs 17:24–41, in which Jews intermarry with a different ethnic group. Though few in number, Samaritans exist in the Middle East today. Many scholars consider the Samaritan religion a pre-Islamic religion.

4). Jesus instinctively tore down the existing the walls he encountered in the first century: race, ethnicity, economics, gender, and most importantly religion (Luke 9:51ff. being one clear example). Part of Jesus' intent on earth was to show his Jewish brothers and sisters how not to kill Samaritans. Or isolate . . . or hate . . . or deem as inferior . . . or engage in *othering*. . . . Jesus didn't stand for any of these options.

There's a growing sentiment among some scholars that first-century Samaritans might, in fact, be considered proto-Muslims who laid the ideological framework for the movement Muhammad started in the sixth century.

I've established the need for this conversation (Christians and Muslims make up half the world's population). I've made the case that Jesus, the Jew, was far more radical and inclusive than many religious people (of all persuasions) in North America are willing to admit. And that this truth has implications for how we think about faith and culture today, Islam and Christianity globally and locally.

Let's get practical.

Real practical.

Because I hope this project influences your church, synagogue, mosque, or interfaith reading group. I hope this project helps you live where you are in a truer, deeper, and more beautiful way.

9

Case Study—Jesus in the City

As I write this, Otter Creek (OC) in Brentwood, Tennessee, is a large (1700 members, 1350 average Sunday attendance), mostly white, highly educated, affluent Church of Christ located in suburban south Nashville, in one of the wealthiest counties in the United States (Williamson County).

I'm the lead teaching minister for this beautiful group of sinners and saints. I often tell my church family, "Eighty percent of you are better followers of the Jesus Way than I am. Twenty percent of you definitely are not. The twenty percent are my job security." It's a deeply spiritual community that doesn't take itself too seriously.

OC has a long history of social engagement dating from its founding in 1929 (the congregation was started by a woman with a heart for forgotten children). During the 1960s, former soldiers and members of the congregation started a college for Korean students that is today a liberal arts university valued at just shy of one billion dollars—Korean Christian University. In the 1970s members of OC started AGAPE, the largest private adoption agency in Nashville. The church followed up by working in the 1980s to help start Room in the Inn—Nashville's largest holistic homeless ministry. Two recent developments in the 1990s and early 2000s are also important to note: first, the formation of the Wayne Reed Center, a school for young children in one of Nashville's poorest neighborhoods, and second, oversight of Made in the Streets, a ministry to bring healing and hope to street children in Nairobi, Kenya. We are in partnership with a local coffeehouse franchise in which we are planting kingdom faith communities within the context of the coffee shop in order to dig water wells around the world.

Otter Creek Church is primed to deal with Christian-Muslim relations because we have been dealing with important cross-cultural conversations from the church's very inception. I share the following with you because my greatest ambition in writing this book is that you would consider implementing real and practical actions to improve the situation between Muslims and Christians in your city. More than simply wanting to write a solid book, I hope you, readers of all backgrounds, will put these words back into flesh in the heart-thumping, creative, keep-you-up-at-night way you know how to do far better than me.

Participatory Action Research

A few years ago, I dedicated five months for a weekly dialogue and discussion group of fifty men and women in my faith community for sixty to ninety minutes. The dialogue group's weekly meeting followed a twofold pattern: intentional teaching and open discussion (thirty minutes each) based mostly upon the issues and ideas presented in the previous chapters. For most of the members of this group, this was their first exposure to a carefully constructed conversation around the subject of Islam and Christianity. Because I was committed to the tenets of participatory action research (PAR), I had no praxis outcome in mind. PAR is an approach to research and study that stresses participation and praxis; it seeks to understand the world by trying to change it, communally and following reflection. PAR emphasizes collective inquiry (as you will see) and experimentation grounded in experience and social history. In fact, experience and social history become paramount for any theological venture with PAR. In some ways, theology cannot be separated from experience or social history.

This was an experiment. I provided the teaching, information, creative stories, and guest speakers, and the rest was up to our group. Here is a summary of the material we covered in the discussion group. I encourage you to try something like this in your circles of influence. If, after reading this book, you think to yourself, *now that's interesting information*, but you don't translate your thoughts into action, then I have failed. If, however, this book inspires you to do something tangible, now we're talking.

Session 1:   Preliminary survey, discussion of inspiration of Scripture, introduction to parables, exploration of Luke 10:25–37, discussion of images and stereotypes.

Session 2:   Recap and discussion of Luke 10, exploration of Isaac and Ishmael in Genesis 16–25, stereotypes in American culture.

Session 3:   Introduction to Islam, the Five Pillars, key issues in linguistics.

Session 4:   Stereotypes in Western Christianity, strategies for engagement.

Session 5:   The Immigration and Nationality Act of 1965 (history and meaning), diversity in America, results of preliminary survey provided.

Session 6:   Exploring the comparison of Samaritans and Jews in the first-century world of Jesus with Muslims and Christians in the twenty-first-century world of the church.

Session 7:   Interview and critical engagement with the Baha'i community of South Nashville and its leader, Aram Ferdowsi.

Session 8:   Interview and critical engagement with Dr. Amir Arain of Vanderbilt University Medical Center and Imam Mohammed Ahmed of the Islamic Center of Nashville.

Session 9:   Case Studies: Masjids and Money; The Cameron Hunt Story.

Session 10:   Where do we go from here? The PAR hits the streets.

Session 11:   Joint dialogue with Nashville Muslims and Christians at the Woodmont Hills Family of God.

Session 12:   Case Study: Park 51 Manhattan Islamic Center.

Session 13:   The Power of Naming One's Narrative: the role of memory, interpretation, experience, and imagination in the life of a religious person.

Discovery

As one primary spiritual voice in this affluent, mostly white Protestant congregation, I brought at least four basic assumptions to this project (previously mentioned) in light of the local context in which I live and for whom I write. Keep in mind that PAR is not a monolithic set of ideas and methods but rather a pluralistic orientation to knowledge-making and social change. The assumptions all of us bring are important. Here are four assumptions I brought to this experiment.

First, many Christians have hard hearts towards Muslims because we do not know any Muslims. That is, many Christians are afraid of Muslims because we lack authentic relationship, deep relationship.

Second, many Christians live such busy lives—caring for children, pursuing education, and working hard—that this entire subject is remarkably intimidating.

Third, many Christians have fallen for dangerous stereotypes that caricature Muslims as backwards, evil, violent, sinister, and deceitful. The terrorist attacks of militant Muslims on 9/11 have been the chief source of this angst and confusion.

Fourth, many Christians feel completely underequipped in engaging persons of different faiths (be they Hindu, or Baha'i, but especially Muslims).

At the onset of the dialogue group, forty men and women were asked to answer the following questions. (See Appendix III for further details.) I encourage you to do a similar study appropriate for your context. Remember, the questions are every bit as important as the answers.

1. When you hear the word *Islam*, what is the first thing that comes to mind?

2. When you hear the word *Muslim*, what is the first thing that comes to mind?

3. When you hear the word *Jew*, what is the first thing that comes to mind?

4. When you sit next to a person of a different ethnicity in a public place (restaurant, airplane, movie theater), do you feel uncomfortable?

5. How many Muslims do you know? Buddhists? Jews? Baha'is? Hindus? Atheists?

6. Do you ever discuss spiritual matters?

7. If Jesus were alive today, what would he look like?

8. How many Muslims do you think live in the U.S.? Buddhists? Jews?

9. Do you see any parallels between being black in the U.S. in the 1960s and being Muslim today?

10. Did you ever notice Muslims before 9/11?

11. What emotions did you experience on 9/11? What emotions did you experience ten years later?

Remember, my aim was to find out if change—*real change*—was possible. I preach lofty, visionary sermons as part of my vocation. But I don't always know if my sermons/teachings have made a difference. This experiment proved that people can actually change. It's not easy, of course, but *difficult* is not the same thing as *impossible*. This experiment proved that attitudes toward and stereotypes about persons of other religious backgrounds could be significantly altered.

Regarding questions 1 and 2: the overwhelming majority (41/50) of the answers were negative and included words such as *crazy, extremist, strange, others,* and *radical.* Surprisingly, the answers to question 3 were much more nuanced and mixed. I believe that Protestant Christians view Jews as allies now that we have a common perceived enemy: Islam. The events of 9/11 had a major impact on those interviewed. The results of the survey can be viewed in Appendix III. All of the survey takers were white Protestants between the ages of twenty-two and sixty-five with high levels of education (bachelor's to doctorate level).

At the conclusion of the thirteen sessions, I offered the same initial survey to the class, most of whom had completely forgotten about it, though it had been given only weeks earlier. The results (also available in Appendix III) were staggering. It is almost as if the entire sample (class members) changed. I cannot underestimate the change in *sight* and *attitude* from late August to early December. This experiment leads me to believe that this material, strategy, and approach can be modeled in evangelical churches across America in urban and suburban contexts with great success. I presented my findings at the Nashville Baha'i Center in 2012. Muslims, Christians, Baha'i, and Buddhists were present.

The following is a summary of the group's conclusions regarding epistemology, orthodoxy, and orthopraxy.

The chief obstacle in creating compassion and understanding between evangelical and mainline Protestants and Muslims is not merely education. The chief issue for both segments of Protestant faith is that too few American Christians know any persons of the Muslim faith. We cannot love whom we do not know. We can only fear. This is our future. What we do with it is up to our leaders.

We base our lives upon stories.

We become the stories we tell ourselves.

We base our values upon the stories we privilege.

We base our beliefs upon those values we try to live.

We base our opinions on the interpretations we assign to various experiences that expose us to the relationship between religion and race, class, and gender.

This is true in marriage, addiction, family secrets, and sports. This is part of what makes humans human. We are the stories we tell ourselves. We also become the new stories we privilege in our lives.

Our interpretations, in turn, inform how we should act. It is a paradoxical cycle filled simultaneously with potential for life, inclusion, understanding, beauty, and hope along with death, exclusion, stereotyping, vilification, and cynicism.

In 2011, this "How *Not* to Kill a Muslim" class/discussion group (which I implore you to try in some form) agreed to the following initiatives (none of which I controlled): twelve members of this class will organize the congregation to participate in an interfaith build for Habitat for Humanity in Nashville. Five members of this class have agreed to create a letter-writing project between children/students at Otter Creek and members of the Islamic community of Nashville. Six members of the class have agreed to birth a table fellowship initiative in which key leaders participate in dinners with key Muslim leaders. In addition, seven members will start a project to get members of the Otter Creek community to visit Amir and Mohammed's mosque on 12th Avenue in Nashville (see Session 8 description above).

As basic as this is, it is the church participating in God's future in the present. The future and the present are always dancing with each other.

10

When Heaven Crashes into Earth

HOPE IS THE MOST powerful act of love we can give to another person. I hope this book is giving you hope; I hope that hope is being birthed in you right now.

The future of Christianity belongs to those who can imagine the world as it will one day be. The answer to the question of this research project—how Christians might engage Muslims in authentic life, conversation, and friendship—is embodied in Cairo, Egypt. Egypt, unlike many countries in the Middle East, has a "historic population of Christians, some 10 percent of the population, who trace their origins back to the Apostle Mark."[1] Moreover, most scholars believe that the man who carried Jesus' cross in Mark's Gospel, Simon of Cyrene, was an African.

On the outer edges of Cairo is a place called Mokkattam. Mokkattam is a sprawling slum near a large garbage dump. The slum, as you can imagine, smells putrid. Out of this unusual place, a vibrant Christian community has emerged. Instead of waging war against their enemies and foes, these Christians are practicing the Jesus Promise that God can use tears to transform societies. Philip Yancey, who went to Mokkattam while in Cairo,

---

1. Yancey, *What Good Is God?*, 206.

calls it "an oasis of beauty in a desert of poverty."[2] Of this "unique community of faith," he writes,

> Led by a priest in the Coptic Orthodox church, the community built houses, schools, a sports field, and a clinic at the foot of a mountain in an abandoned quarry. Around thirty years ago one of the slum dwellers stumbled across a large cave, and over time Coptic Christians moved one hundred forty thousand tons of rock out of the cave to form a three-thousand-seat auditorium. They worked mostly at night during Muslim fast periods, when the guards who might harass them went home to eat.[3]

The witness of the Coptic church is essential for American Christians reading this book. Christians in America are called to give American Muslims the same dignity and respect they would like to see given to their fellow Christians in Egypt. That is, the United States is majority Christian, while Egypt is majority Muslim. The U.S. has a minority population of Muslims. Egypt has a minority population of Christians. While it's easy to be inspired by the Coptic Christian faithfulness to suffering love, there's a deeper question about how the powerful engage and care for the less powerful.[4]

Every week, Christian churches in America—black, white, Latino, and Asian, as well as Methodist, Baptist, nondenominational, Catholic, Episcopal, Churches of Christ—come together and sing praises to God. But most weeks, when we sing praises, we do so as individuals coming from different places. We sing them from the place of a new job, unexpected pregnancy, or confirmation of God's presence. But we also sing praises from our dark places—the mother who buried her son when he was five, the father of three whose wife left without the decency of a note, the unexpected divorce in the model family. We have to sing from those places too, because both the peaks and valleys are what make us human.

The real question is this: Why are we afraid to be the humans God made us to be? Because engaging our Muslim neighbor is not just about Muslims; it is about Christians becoming the people God desires us to be.

The demonstration plot that is the Coptic community of Mokkattam, apprenticed to the Jesus Way, has grown considerably. Currently the church now meets in a facility described as a thirteen-thousand-seat amphitheater,

2. Ibid.

3. Ibid., 207–8.

4. For a mind-bending twist on this kind of thinking, see Giridharadas, *The True American*.

also carved out of rock. It is, without any question, the largest Christian community in the entire Middle East. Out of a garbage pit, *life*. Out of death, *resurrection*. Through tears, *healing*.

See this community of believers.

Can you imagine the worship experience of thirteen thousand Egyptian Christians who have known suffering, isolation, marginalization, and oppression? They do not sing because they have *avoided* suffering and pain. They sing as we sing, because we experienced something holy, had it named, and still believe that God is moving in the world, preparing us for the great mystery of God's new heaven and new earth. We need more of *this* in North America.

In my most recent publication, *Heaven on Earth*, I implore contemporary Christians to reclaim a passion for peacemaking in real situations of violence; I believe that when we pursue this calling, we participate in bringing heaven to earth.[5] By far, the chapter on peacemaking created the most confusion and elicited the greatest response and emotion from readers. I'm confident I tapped into a larger reality—the work of people of faith in bringing the peace of God from heaven to earth in this present dimension.

Here's what it looks like theologically and practically. I hope this becomes the hope you take into all the places of violence, tension, hate, and mistrust you find yourself in.

Peacemaking is the intentional decision to participate in God's future (the shalom of God) in the present. Peacemaking often shows up in counterintuitive ways. Peacemaking is radical trust in the absurdity of God and the cross over the certainty of power, violence, and revenge. Theologian Donald Hagner writes, "In the context of the beatitudes, the point would seem to be directed against the Zealots, the Jewish revolutionaries who hoped through violence to bring the kingdom of God. Such means would have been a continual temptation for the downtrodden and oppressed who longed for the kingdom. The Zealots by their militarism hoped furthermore to demonstrate that they were loyal 'sons of God.' But Jesus announces . . . it is the peacemakers who will be called 'children of God.'"[6]

---

5. See chapter 8, "The Road to Peace," in Seidman and Graves, *Heaven on Earth*, 87–101. The following is an altered version of that chapter.

6. Hagner, *Matthew 1–13*, 94. In a recent private lecture, N. T. Wright made the point that the early church in the Roman Empire was an *ekklesia* of intentional reconciliation. That is, the early church was a collection of intentional gatherings practicing peace in the midst of social, ethnic, religious, and class division.

Peace is not simply the avoidance of war. Peace is the intentional conversation, the shared experience, the recognition of commonality between warring individuals and communities; it is the work of people who wake up one day and decide to be brokers of reconciliation.

One difficulty in believing Hagner can be put in the form of a question about how one reads the Bible: Do you begin reading the story of God in scripture in Genesis 1 or Genesis 3? That is, do you read the story, and your own life, through the lens of the power, creativity, goodness, and imagination of God (Gen 1) or do you read the story through the lens of sin, chaos, rebellion, violence, and death (Gen 3)?

If you begin reading the story in the wrong place, you might end up in the wrong place. Had Jesus started in Genesis 3, he would not have been able to tell Luke 10.

Because the essence of Christianity is not so much that Jesus is like God; the scandal of Christian faith lies in the belief that *God is like Jesus.* If it cannot be said of Jesus, then it can no longer be said of God (if it ever could have been in the first place). Paul puts it like this: "Jesus is the image of the invisible of God" (Col 1:15). The writer of Hebrews captures this truth: "Jesus is the exact reflection of God's glory and the exact imprint of God's very being, and he sustains all things by his powerful word" (Heb 1:3).

Jewish and Christian theologians commonly recognize the belief that Genesis 1 and 2 describe the peace of God or the *shalom* of God. Furthermore, many Jewish theologians today note that so much of Torah is concerned with helping humanity reclaim the good and whole relationship—the shalom of God—as experienced in the very beginning of the story.

Theologian Cornelius Plantinga describes the shalom of God thusly:

> The webbing together of God, humans, and all creation in justice, fulfillment, and delight is what the Hebrew prophets call *shalom.* We call it peace, but it means far more than mere peace of mind or a cease-fire between enemies. In the Bible, shalom means *universal flourishing, wholeness, and delight*—a rich state of affairs in which natural needs are satisfied and natural gifts fruitfully employed, a state of affairs that inspires joyful wonder as its Creator and Savior opens doors and welcomes the creatures in whom he delights. Shalom, in other words, is the way things ought to be.[7]

7. Plantinga, *Not the Way It's Supposed to Be*, 10. For all the multiple connections of peace and the people of God, see Gen 43:27; Exod 4:18; 1 Kgs 5:12; Ps 85:10; 122:6; Isa

Shalom and peace mean . . .

To make peace.

To restore.

To make whole.

Many consider *peace* no more than the absence of conflict. In Jewish teaching, shalom is much bigger. It's an imaginative exercise of epic proportion.[8]

Isaiah 65:17–25 is perhaps the strongest Old Testament fulfillment of the coming of the *shalom* (peace) of God as found in the person. *Fulfilled* meaning, of course, that Jesus filled this text *full of meaning.*

> "See, I will create
> new heavens and a new earth.
> The former things will not be remembered,
> nor will they come to mind.
> But be glad and rejoice forever
> in what I will create,
> for I will create Jerusalem to be a delight
> and its people a joy.
> I will rejoice over Jerusalem
> and take delight in my people;
> the sound of weeping and of crying
> will be heard in it no more.
>
> "Never again will there be in it
> an infant who lives but a few days,
> or an old man who does not live out his years;
> the one who dies at a hundred
> will be thought a mere child;
> the one who fails to reach a hundred

2:2–4; 9:6; 11:1–9; 48:18, 22; 57:19–21; Jer 29:7; Mic 5:4–5a; Hag 2:7–9.

8. Jesus viewed the world through the lens of Genesis 1 and 2. Much of his kingdom mission was to usher in an age that faithfully reflected the world described in Genesis 1 and 2. It is not too much of a stretch to suggest that Genesis was the gospel Jesus read and lived by. Genesis was the script that funded Jesus' imagination. Jesus believed in the authority (Gen 1:2), power (Gen 1:1–3), and creativity/imagination of God (Gen 1–2). Jesus also believed in Genesis' fundamentally radical claims concerning the goodness of creation (1:4, 10, 12, 18, 21, 25, 31) and the divinity that every human bears (1:26ff). How else, for instance, could Jesus offer the two pillar teachings of Luke 10 (The Merciful Samaritan) and Luke 15 (Prodigal Son) if not for the latter?

will be considered accursed.
They will build houses and dwell in them;
    they will plant vineyards and eat their fruit.
No longer will they build houses and others live in them,
    or plant and others eat.
For as the days of a tree,
    so will be the days of my people;
my chosen ones will long enjoy
    the work of their hands.
They will not labor in vain,
    nor will they bear children doomed to misfortune;
for they will be a people blessed by the LORD,
    they and their descendants with them.
Before they call I will answer;
    while they are still speaking I will hear.
The wolf and the lamb will feed together,
    and the lion will eat straw like the ox,
    and dust will be the serpent's food.
They will neither harm nor destroy
    on all my holy mountain,"
    says the LORD.

One of the key aims of Jesus—often lost on modern-day audiences—was to show Israel the path to co-creating the shalom of God in their present circumstances. His way of doing this, the kingdom of God, often came into sharp conflict with the Jewish and Roman authorities of the day. Peacemaking was at the heart of all that Jesus was attempting to set in motion.

The *shalom* of God is a constant theme in the New Testament, where key scriptures like Revelation 21–22 and Romans 8 all describe and invite the shalom of God.[9] In fact, "peace" is the common greeting in most of the New Testament letters.[10]

Jesus captures the Jewish passion for peace and shalom, and the remaining pages of the New Testament must be interpreted through this vision.

For example, in the seventh Beatitude, "Blessed are the peacemakers," Jesus provides a foreshadowing of his own destiny: to show forth heaven on earth. His life and death become a public parable of that which he's already expressed in the teaching. His life is the meaning of the Beatitude.

9. See also Luke 2:14; John 14:27; 20:19; Acts 10:36; Rom 16:20; and Rev 6:4.

10. Rom 1:7; Col 1:2; 1 Cor 1:3; 2 Cor 1:2; Eph 1:2; Phil 1:2; 1 Thess 1:1; Titus 1:4; 1 Pet 1:2; 2 Pet 1:2; 2 John 1:3; Jude 1:2; Rev 1:4.

New Testament scholar Charles Campbell points out that Jesus' triumphal entry into Jerusalem, in Matt 21:1–11, is street theater. Jesus is performing a *Saturday Night Live* parody of the ways in which Herod and Caesar strolled into cities they controlled through power and violence. Jesus is literally playing the fool in order to suggest a different way of leading and loving—peacemaking in the here and now. "The whole time, however, he is turning the world's notion of power, rule, and kingship on their head. His theater is a wonderful piece of political satire. . . . The event takes on the air of a carnival, where those on the bottom of society festively unmask and challenge the dominant social order."[11] Campbell goes on to argue that "Blessed are the peacemakers" becomes a living word that animates the entire Sermon on the Mount. In this new community, this new way of being human, Jesus dares his listeners to imagine a world that appears to be foolish.[12]

Campbell says that foolishness is required for believing *in* and *bringing* shalom to a world marred by suspicion, greed, violence, animosity, rivalry, and hate. The question is, do we really think Jesus knew what he was talking about? Can we really pursue peace in a violent world? What would it look like if we did?

The Gospel of Matthew—the larger Jesus Story—doesn't leave us to wonder. Throughout the First Gospel, the writer gives us clear snapshots of Jesus embodying what he meant in this Beatitude.[13] The entire passion

11. Campbell, "Folly of the Sermon on the Mount," 60.

12. Reconciliation is more important than vengeance (5:21–26); women are no longer treated as objects (5:27–32); enemies are loved not destroyed (5:38–48); religious practices are not about superiority (6:1–18); desire for wealth is not the prime motivation in life (6:19–34).

13. If you want to know what Jesus meant when he said that "peacemakers are children of God," consider what he taught and how he lived. Matthew's larger story lays this out in easy-to-follow fashion: Jesus' birth is a threat to the Roman government, which keeps its version of "peace" through violence and bullying (1:18—2:23). Fast-forward to his time in the wilderness, where he resists the tactics of Satan, demonstrating that he will be a suffering king, not a king who needs power to rule (4:1–11; 20:17–28). Then Jesus begins to teach his disciples that his suffering will become their suffering (10:16–23). That is, the commitment to peacemaking is not for Jesus alone but for anyone bold enough to wear his name and proclaim his kingdom project. Matthew's Gospel also gives us a glimpse of a minor but important character, John the Baptist, as a faithful sufferer committed to Jesus' peacemaking project (14:1–12). Jesus again reiterates the necessity of suffering on behalf of others—peacemaking for a purpose (16:21–28; 17:22–23). Instead of advocating revenge or harm against one who has wronged you, Jesus encourages his disciples to practice peacemaking through reconciliation (18:15–35).

narrative—the willingness of Jesus to suffer as a means to peace—should be considered Jesus' ultimate commitment to showing the truth of the Beatitude that peacemaking is what God's children do. The kingdom and the cross can't be separated (Matt 26–28). It is in this setting that Jesus says, after one of his own disciple's attempts to answer violence with violence, "Put your sword away, for all who take the sword, perish by the sword" (26:52).

Lee Camp summarizes the redemptive role of intentional suffering when he writes, "The 'crucified God' stands in judgment upon the kings, the corporations, the nations, the emperors, the rulers, the presidents, the prime ministers of this world who seek violently to wield power, to control and dominate."[14] Jesus demonstrates the true path to peace.

Jesus' kingdom project was an extension of the peace project of Torah and the prophets. This is why peace is such a prominent word and concept in the New Testament. Peacemaking is central to almost every single narrative/text in Scripture.[15]

The careful reader of Matthew's Jesus Story often asks this question: If Jesus' mission in announcing the kingdom of God is to somehow participate in the Jewish belief in the shalom of God, why did Jesus clearly state, in Matthew, that he did not come to *bring peace to earth* but that he came to *bring a sword* (10:34)? Read in context, the answer is clear: Jesus is addressing the human propensity to be comfortable, to play it safe, to avoid taking a risk (cf. Matt 25:14–30). The gospel message is dangerous. It's countercultural. It might even cost you your life. For anyone to play Matt 10:34 as a trump card in favor of violence, ignoring the numerous passages previously mentioned, is irresponsible at best.

If anyone desires to know what Jesus meant when he said, "Blessed are the peacemakers, for they will be called children of God," all he or she has to do is watch how Jesus lived and consider what he taught. Because how he lived and what he taught is what he meant when he invited women and men to apprentice themselves to his movement, the kingdom of God, ushering in a new era, with new values and new ways of seeing. Can we

14. Camp, *Mere Discipleship*, 106.

15. A few more examples: Rom 14:19, "Let us therefore make every effort to what leads to peace and mutual edification"; Heb 12:14, "Make every effort to live in peace with everyone "; Eph 6:15, where, in the middle of a teaching on the powers and principalities, Paul refers to the gospel as the "gospel of peace"; James 3:18, "Peacemakers who sow in peace reap a harvest of righteousness"; 1 Pet 3:11, "They must turn from evil and do good; they must seek peace and pursue it."

agree that Christianity should stand against all violence, fear, hate, and exploitation toward our Muslim neighbors?

Let's tear down the walls, shall we? Let's stop killing (and the justification of killing), stop the hate, isolation, shaming, suspicion, malice, and strife. Let's get on with the courageous business of being like Jesus.

Stop killing. Stop hating. Stop driving the wedge deeper.

11

When Heaven Crashes into New York City (St. Paul's Miracle)

I'm a believer, but religion is the thing when God, like Elvis, has left the building. But when God is in the house, you get something else. I'm happy in a Catholic cathedral or a tent show down in the South with gospel music.

—Bono

MANY READERS OF THIS book are leaders in churches, synagogues, and university settings. You are pastors, elders, ministry leaders, writers, scholars, shapers, thinkers, doers, and persons of influence. Some of you lead vibrant, effective communities of faith or important not-for-profit organizations. Are you considering the role of worship and action, contemplation and engagement, the role of the church in the midst of a city?

Here's a theological roadmap for bringing this conversation from the head (book) to the heart (life of a local church).

New York City is one of the more interesting places in the world. It is the ethnic melting pot of the Eastern Seaboard, not to mention the fact that fashion and philosophical trends in the United States must first flow through the Big Apple before making their way westward.

New York also boasts some of the most interesting churches in the United States. The aura of Riverside Church in uptown Manhattan blew me away the first time I walked in and contemplated its history. Founded by the Rockefeller family, Riverside (formerly known as Riverside Baptist Church) is one of the most important churches in recent American history. It was the home of one of the twentieth century's greatest preachers, Harry Emerson Fosdick. That name might not mean much to some, yet Fosdick influenced whole generations of black and white preachers all around the world.

Dr. Martin Luther King Jr. delivered some of his most important sermons at Riverside during the civil rights movement.[1] It was after one of his trips to Riverside that John F. Kennedy and Dr. King met for the first time, forever changing the course of American politics: in 1956 the majority of African Americans voted Republican, but in 1960 the majority of African Americans voted Democratic. To illustrate how large a shift this was, consider a shift of similar size and significance that more of us can remember: the white, conservative Christian "Moral Majority" that voted for Ronald Reagan in 1980. When I consider its past, I can only conclude that Riverside Church is not merely a building; it is a people who've played an integral role in the American story.

Israel had her own religiously, historically, and socially important center for worship during the life of Jesus. Many know this holy space as the temple but it was also known as the house of worship, God's House, and the dwelling place of God. The temple was not just metaphorically important, for it took up almost 25 percent of Jerusalem proper at that time. Jerusalem was not so much a city with a temple in it; it was rather more like a temple with a small city around it, to paraphrase one church historian.

Close to Times Square and Rockefeller Center stands St. Patrick's Cathedral: an icon in the American religious landscape. Church leaders, entrepreneurs, famous athletes, and entertainers are married and buried here. A security guard asked me to take off my winter cap, as a sign of respect, as I stepped inside. I completely understood, but at that same moment a woman walked by with her cocker spaniel. I looked at the guy and shrugged. He gave me a look back as if to say *There's nothing I can do—dogs don't wear hats.*

Important people gravitated toward the temple as well. Josephus, a contemporary of Jesus and Paul, described the temple as a "mountain of

1. See Richard Lischer's *The Preacher King* as well as Taylor Branch's trilogy: *Parting the Waters*, *Pillar of Fire*, and *At Canaan's Edge*. Excellent online resources include the website of The King Center (http://www.thekingcenter.org) and NPR's "The Speeches of Martin Luther King Jr." (http://www.npr.org/news/specials/march40th/speeches.html).

snow" as it glittered in the sunlight. He also captured the attitudes of the everyday Jew by summarizing their temple philosophy, saying, "We have but one temple for the one God."[2] The temple was the space where heaven and earth, God and humanity, intersected.

While in New York City, I was interested in visiting one more church: Brooklyn Tabernacle, located in the heart of Brooklyn. I first learned about this church when its pastor, Jim Cymbala, came to a local Nashville church located near the seminary I was attending. Cymbala had a vision to build and grow a truly diverse church that represented the ethnicity of the borough of Brooklyn.

Today, after starting with a few families in a rented facility, Brooklyn Tabernacle is a church of several thousand, often considered the most diverse church in the United States. Over the last ten years, I've taken a group of students to one of their prayer services for a powerful hour and a half of intercessory prayer. There is no praying for the hands and minds of the doctors—*they pray in the authority and power of Jesus for healing*. It is interesting how those two words function in churches comprised of minorities: *authority* and *power*. Some leading church thinkers tell us that the more the church is pushed to the margins of our Western "church-fatigued" culture, the more crucial it is that churches demonstrate the power and authority of Jesus over against all other powers and authorities.

The reason I've walked you through these three contemporary temples is to illustrate what would have been perfectly clear to ancient Israel. First, the temple was the one entity within Israel that was a visible demonstration of God's faithfulness and their place within human history. It was the one thing that said to the world, *We matter; we have a story and a God who is above all other gods*. The temple was the epicenter of Israel's life and very existence. Second, the temple was the center of *religious life*. This was the place where sins were forgiven, justice announced, and relationship restored. It was also the place where people gathered for the important meals and feasts of the Jewish calendar. Third, the temple was the center of *educational life*. It was where one learned to read Torah and to rehearse the practices central to Judaism. Fourth, the temple was the center of *Jewish government*. It was the headquarters for the high priest, the leader who stood between Rome

2. The work of Everett Ferguson greatly influences this section. See Ferguson, *Backgrounds of Early Christianity*, 527–30. Ferguson writes, "The temple, as other Near Eastern sanctuaries, served as a depository for keeping valuables. Hence, Jesus' action in cleansing the temple looked revolutionary. It was an assault on the economic system and a challenge to the position of the temple authorities" (530).

and Jerusalem, walking the political tightrope of loyalty to Jewish customs and allegiance to Caesar. (It was quite a tight rope.) Fifth, the temple was *the center of finance and economics*. The temple tax was a staple in the economic vitality of Jewish religious life. And finally, the temple was also the slaughterhouse for the animals brought to be sacrificed.

To summarize, the temple was a combination of Wall Street, the White House, Harvard, and the Washington Cathedral. It was the heart that pushed blood to all corners of Israel, providing life, sustenance, and meaning.

Christianity and the Temple

It is therefore crucial to understand how Jesus, then Paul and Luke, take on the prevailing attitudes or *temple theology*. Eat all of *these* words.

Jesus is quoted in the first three Gospels as saying (in reference to himself), "Tear down the temple and I'll rebuild it in three days [John 2:19]; something greater than the temple is here [Matt 12:6]." The Jews had been working on the temple for several generations—who does this guy think he is? He's going for the jugular of all Jewish faith. Stephen reminded a crowd of Jewish listeners, "however, the Most High does not live in houses made by men" (Acts 7:48). Paul picks up on these teachings of Jesus and uses temple language in describing the church: "In view of God's mercy, to offer yourselves as living sacrifices, holy and pleasing to God—this is your act of spiritual worship" (Rom 12:1). "Don't you know that you yourselves are God's temple and that God's Spirit lives in you?" (1 Cor 3:16). "For we are the temple of the living God. As God has said: 'I will live with them and walk among them, and I will be their God, and they will be my people'" (2 Cor 6:16). "And in him you too are being built together to become a dwelling in which God lives by his Spirit" (Eph 2:22).

Even a cursory reading of the New Testament paints a compelling picture of the early church as a collection of women and men empowered by the Holy Spirit. They met in homes, synagogue, public places—wherever they met, there the church existed. The earliest followers of Jesus worshipped together, broke bread (the Lord's Supper), and told stories about their Messiah. The early church often remembered what we so easily forget: the church gathers in order to be sent. This is not to downplay the mystical relationship between the space and the people but to remember that ultimately God's purposes in the world are accomplished through people—not brick and mortar.

Temple Mentality

The modern American church—especially in suburbia—often slips back into this *particular temple mentality*. God was not content to be bound by a street address in the life of Israel. It is so easy for Christians to slip into what some Jewish persons fell prey to in the first-century world. Instead of seeing God among us as a people, we relegate and confine the presence of God to a building or a holy place.[3]

Let me give you three examples.

First: Many look upon the church as a *physical location*. I'm flying back to Detroit after speaking at a conference in Orlando. The woman I'm sitting next to politely asks, "So, young man, what do you do for a living?"

"Well, I'm a pastor of a church," I reply.

"Oh, that's lovely. I'm a Christian too. Say, *where is* your church located? I'd like to come *to* your church."

While not a disastrous reality (after all, I believe in sacred spaces), our language betrays us.

Second, some view the church as a *center for the distribution of goods and services*, as if the church is nothing more than a spiritual Home Depot. "I need my kids to get spirituality mixed in with everything else." "We're getting married in a church." "His funeral must be performed in the church where he was baptized." The church is one more place in the marketplace to meet one's needs. Sears, Burger King, Home Depot . . . now, the *local church*.

Third, some Christians are more passionate about what happens on *Sunday morning* (in the temple!) than the ministry taking place during the rest of the week. This can be equally true of staunch conservative churches and cutting-edge, culturally savvy progressive churches.

St. Paul's: Radical Islam Meets Manhattan

I'm not claiming that the gathered assembly lacks power or meaning. That is not true of my own experience as a Christian. There is great power in

---

3. Rob Warner also discusses "temple mentality" in his book *21st Century Church*, 127–30.

the gathered assembly; I've seen lives changed, hearts renewed, and soul's pierced as a result of the public assembly.

The gathered assembly, however, is only *part* of the story. The people of God gather in order to be sent. If the people of God gather for the sake of gathering, they are no longer the people of God. It is when the church gathers in order to be sent back out into the world that our understanding of worship takes on whole new possibilities.

Imagine this from a different vantage point.

There's another church in New York City I have not taken you to . . . yet. This church is not a megachurch, but it is one that has accomplished profound ministry. It is St. Paul's Chapel, located right across from Ground Zero in the heart of Manhattan. St. Paul's is Manhattan's oldest public building in continuous use. It also has played an intriguing role in American history.

George Washington worshiped here on Inauguration Day, April 30, 1789, and attended services at St. Paul's during the two years in which New York City was the nation's capital. Above his pew is an eighteenth-century oil painting of the Great Seal of the United States, which was adopted in 1782.

Directly across the chapel is the Governor's pew, which George Clinton, the first governor of the state of New York, used when he visited St. Paul's. The Arms of the State of New York are on the wall above the pew.

Other well-known players in Western history who worshiped at St. Paul's Chapel include Prince William, King William IV of England, and Lord Cornwallis, who is most famous in this country for surrendering at the Battle of Yorktown in 1781.

When the World Trade Center Towers came crashing down that dark day almost fifteen years ago, St. Paul's was the only building in the immediate area still functional and *functioning*. St. Paul's is not an impressive structure per se. I've stood inside it multiple times over the last few years. It is rather quaint and old. Yet it played a crucial role in the aftermath of 9/11. Here's how the church describes the events.[4]

After the attacks of September 11, 2001, which led to the collapse of the Twin Towers of the World Trade Center, St. Paul's Chapel served as a place of rest and refuge for recovery workers at the WTC site.

For eight months, hundreds of volunteers worked twelve-hour shifts around the clock, serving meals, making beds, counseling and praying with fire fighters, construction workers, police officers, and others. Massage

4. See http://www.saintpaulschapel.org/video/trinity-staff-recall-9-11.

therapists, chiropractors, podiatrists, and musicians likewise tended to their needs.

The folks at St. Paul's could have started a "purify America" or a "real America" rally—or a movement based upon fear and revenge. But they didn't, because they remembered who they were. They had a story. A better story. As the world around them was in shambles, they became a place where people gathered in order to be sent back out. They took the pew where George Washington once sat and turned it into an area for volunteer workers to massage the feet of firefighters who were working sixteen-hour shifts. St. Paul's understood at a deep, mystical level that the church is a people not a place.

Fire, devastation, destruction, and death were swallowing hundreds of people right outside their building. Instead of retreating or creating a country club, they opened their arms and hearts as wide as Jesus did on the cross, saying, *All are welcome in this place. But know this. If you come in here, you will be sent back out to bring in the weary, fatigued, worn-down, and broken.* While everyone was running away from the chaos of Ground Zero, the folks of St. Paul's ran toward the death and carnage.

The church is gathered *to be sent*. We come to our sacred gathering as an actor comes to rehearsal. We receive our script (the Gospel) and then return to the unfolding drama to play our parts as actors who represent the more excellent way of our Lord Jesus.[5]

Christians have been empowered to continue to live out God's story, a story that is incomplete without actors to practice spirit-filled improvisation. A story that begs for *improv* actors, men and women courageous enough to imagine what Christianity might look like in our complex world today.

5. One of my favorite thinkers points to this same truth in a story about a Mozart music mystery. "One day, rummaging through a dusty old attic in a small Austrian town, a collector comes across a faded manuscript containing many pages of music. It is written for the piano. Curious, he takes it to a dealer. The dealer phones a friend, who appears half an hour later. When he sees the music he becomes excited, then puzzled. This looks like the handwriting of Mozart himself, but it isn't a well-known piece. In fact, he's never heard it. More phone calls. More excitement. More consultations. It really does seem to be Mozart. And, though some parts seem distantly familiar, it doesn't correspond to anything already known in his works. . . . What they are looking at is indeed by Mozart. It is indeed beautiful. But it's the piano part of a piece that involves another instrument, or perhaps other instruments. By itself it is frustratingly incomplete. A further search of the attic reveals nothing else that would provide a clue. The piano music is all there is, a signpost to something that was there once and might still turn up one day." See Wright, *Simply Christian*, 39–40.

There's a Jewish tradition out of Genesis that we need to pay attention to in order to faithfully embody the good news of everything I've just laid out. The tradition is often referred to as *Tikkun Olam* (pronounced tea-*koon* oh-*lahm*). In English, it simply means "to repair the world." In the beginning God created the world, but the world is longer the one that God created (that's a succinct summary of Genesis 1, 2, *and* 3). This tradition says that something happened to shatter the light of the universe into countless pieces. Trillions of light particles became lodged as miniscule sparks inside every facet of creation. Leonard Cohen captured this truth with the lyric, "There's a crack, a crack in everything. That's how the light gets in."

A'vodah (a-vo-*dah*) is the transliteration of a Hebrew word that can be used to mean both work and worship. It is used to describe human work in Exod 34:21 and Prov 12:11. It is also used to describe the intentional worship of God in Psa 72:11, Josh 24:15, and Exod 8:1. John 5:17 summarizes this beautifully: God is always at work.

We are people of worship and work in service to God and to each other.

It's that simple.

It's that hard.

While many run from Islam, or from poverty, immigration, AIDS, third-world debt relief, the church runs *toward* them all. It is a dangerous mission. But it is the mission to which God has called us. In our baptism, he calls us to a life of search and rescue. Each time we gather, we do so with the full knowledge that we are *being sent*.

Sent to usher in *the shalom of God*, to bring shalom to every person, space, and place. The first step in not killing your Muslim neighbor is to join a church that reads the gospels (particularly Luke 10) *and* puts those words into action.

We're moving beyond stereotypes. The future depends upon it.

Beyond fear. Beyond anger. Beyond rage. Beyond caricatures.

So be bold. And do not be afraid.

The following prayer from Bishop Ken Untener seems the most fitting way to end this conversation:

It helps, now and then, to step back and take a long view. The Kingdom of God is not only beyond our efforts, it is even beyond our vision. We accomplish in our lifetime only a tiny fraction of the magnificent enterprise that is God's work. Nothing we do is complete, which is a way of saying that the Kingdom always lies beyond us.

No statement says all that could be said. No prayer fully expresses our faith. No confession brings perfection, no pastoral visit brings wholeness. No program accomplishes the Church's mission. No set of goals and objectives includes everything.

This is what we are about. We plant the seeds that one day will grow. We water seeds already planted knowing that they hold future promise. We lay foundations that will need further development. We provide yeast that produces effects far beyond our capabilities. We cannot do everything, and there is a sense of liberation in realizing this. This enables us to do something, and to do it very well.

It may be incomplete, but it is a beginning, a step along the way, an opportunity for the Lord's grace to enter and do the rest. We may never see the end results, but that is the difference between the master builder and the worker. We are workers, not master builders; ministers not messiahs. We are prophets of a future not our own.[6]

6. "Reflection on Ministry" (often called the "Archbishop Romero Prayer"), in Untener, *Practical Prophet*, iii.

Appendix I

Islam for Dummies (Like Me)

Note: Since I began teaching, writing, and researching the relationship of Islam and Christianity globally and domestically, I have been constantly aware of (and befuddled by!) the general lack of knowledge of the basic tenets of Islam. So, I offer the following as a cheat sheet or basic review of the major elements (beliefs, leaders, etc.) of Islam. You can use this the next time you are breaking bread or sharing coffee with a Muslim friend. Or the next time you find yourself in a controversial Thanksgiving family fight on religion and politics. #youarewelcome

Abraham: One of the biblical patriarchs and the father of the Abrahamic religions: Judaism, Christianity, and Islam. According to Genesis, Abraham and God enter into a covenant. Although Abraham is old and his wife, Sarah, is barren, God promises to make him the father of a great nation residing in a promised land, and Abraham agrees in turn to circumcise his male children. Abraham is best known for obeying God's command to sacrifice his son, Isaac. After Abraham bound Isaac on an altar and raised a knife to slay him, an angel stayed his hand and a nearby ram was sacrificed instead. Abraham is also revered by Christians, who see him as a person of great faith, and by Muslims, who call him Ibrahim and cite the story of the binding of his son (not Isaac but Ishmael—*Ismail* in Arabic—according to

Muslims) to support their view of Abraham as the first Muslim and their understanding of themselves as heirs of his promises (including the land of Canaan). Toward the end of the twentieth century, and particularly after the events of September 11, 2001, Americans began to speak of Judaism, Christianity, and Islam as Abrahamic religions. In September 2002, Abraham appeared on the cover of *Time* magazine as the father of these faiths.

Allah: Term for God in Arabic and Islam. In the Qur'an, Allah is described as merciful, gracious, and compassionate and is said to be the creator, sustainer, ruler, judge, and redeemer of the universe. Muslims traditionally ascribe to God ninety-nine beautiful names, including *The Just*, *The Mighty*, and *The Perfectly Wise*. The most important teaching about Allah, however, is *tawhid*, or divine oneness, a view inscribed in the Shahadah, or Muslim creed, as "There is no God but God." Rival understandings of God, including polytheism and the Christian view that God is somehow three in one, Muslims reject as *shirk*, or ascribing partners to Allah (who alone is divine).

Al-Qaeda: International terrorist organization founded in the late 1980s by the wealthy Saudi-born financier Osama bin Laden (b. 1957). Al-Qaeda is best known for hijacking four jets on September 11, 2001, and crashing them into the World Trade Center, the Pentagon, and a Pennsylvania field. Influenced by Wahhabism and other forms of Islamist thought, al-Qaeda (meaning "The Base") emerged in 1986 out of an organization bin Laden used to finance the struggle of the Mujahideen (holy warriors) against Soviet occupation of Afghanistan—a struggle funded in part by the United States. After the Soviet withdrawal, completed in February 1989, al-Qaeda enjoyed safe haven in Afghanistan under the Taliban, a theocratic Sunni state that punished theft by amputation, banned television, and mandated that women wear the *burqa* (a veil covering the entire body) in public. From that base al-Qaeda launched a holy war against Western occupation of Muslim lands, especially the presence of American troops in Saudi Arabia. That jihad, as members called it, proceeds on two fronts: against the *near enemy* Muslim-majority states—Saudi Arabia chief among them—that it regards as apostate, and against the *far enemy* of the United States and other Western powers that support those apostate regimes.

Bin Laden, Osama (b. 1957; d. 2011): Saudi-born head of the international terrorist organization al-Qaeda, one of the CIA's most wanted men, and a Che Guevara–style hero to many Muslim youth. Bin Laden inherited considerable wealth when his father, a Yemeni construction magnate, died in 1968. In 1979 bin Laden went to Afghanistan to fight with the Mujahideen against Soviet occupation of that Muslim-majority nation. He later founded and financed a Sunni organization devoted to this cause, which would evolve into al-Qaeda ("The Base"). Upon returning to Saudi Arabia after the Soviets withdrew from Afghanistan, bin Laden became incensed when, following the 1990 Iraqi invasion of Kuwait, the home to Islam's two most sacred cities. Expelled from Saudi Arabia he moved to Sudan in 1991. Expelled by the Sudanese in 1996, he found safe haven in Afghanistan under the Taliban, a theocratic Sunni state. That same year he declared a holy war against U.S. forces. Two years later he issued a so-called *fatwa*, "Jihad Against Jews and Crusaders," in which he referred to American soldiers as "crusader armies spreading in [the Arabian Peninsula] like locusts, eating its riches" and urged all Muslims "to kill the Americans and their allies—civilian and military." Bin Laden has been linked to terrorist attacks in many different countries, but none as devastating as the September 11, 2001, attacks that killed thousands of people in New York City, Washington, DC, and rural Pennsylvania—including some sixty American Muslims. Following these attacks the United States military invaded Afghanistan, uprooting the Taliban and forcing bin Laden into hiding. After 9/11 he appeared on a series of video and audio tapes.

Black Muslims or Nation of Islam: Members of the black nationalist sect the Nation of Islam (NOI), founded in Detroit in the 1930s by W. D. Fard and led today by Louis Farrakhan (b. 1933). Under the leadership of Elijah Muhammad (1897–1975), who spearheaded this group after Fard's disappearance in 1934, the NOI preached a heterodox combination of black nationalism and Islam that denounced whites as blue-eyed devils and hoped for a separate black nation. More traditional Muslims looked askance at the Black Muslims' doctrines (e.g., the view that Fard was divine) and practices (e.g., fasting in December instead of Ramadan), but the movement grew throughout the 1960s, particularly among black males in prisons, who gravitated to its strict discipline and its emphasis on self-help and self-respect. One prison convert was Malcolm X (1925–65), who before his assassination in 1965 represented the most powerful alternative to the more moderate civil rights leader Reverend Martin Luther King Jr. His autobiography (*The Autobiography of Malcolm X*, with Alex Haley) is considered one of the most important works of the twentieth century. The most famous convert to the Nation of Islam was the heavyweight boxing champion Cassius Clay, who in 1964 proclaimed his conversion to Islam and changed his name to Muhammad Ali.

The Crusades: Medieval military campaigns of the eleventh through the fifteenth centuries waged by Christians to recapture the Holy Lands from Muslims. The church offered indulgences for the remission of sins to Crusaders, as Christian participants were called, and lauded as martyrs those who died in these "holy wars." Although successful militarily, the Crusades badly damaged Christian-Muslim relations, precipitating an era of mistrust and hostility that continues to characterize their relations today. In September 2001 President George W. Bush referred to the war on terrorism as a "crusade," sparking anger among Muslims aware of the history of medieval crusades and the religious meaning of the term as "taking the cross." Ayman al-Zawahiri, the current leader of al-Qaeda, has called the war on terror Bush's "new Crusade against Islam."

Eid: This term, Arabic for *feast*, refers to two festivals in the Muslim calendar: Eid al-Fitr, the feast of the breaking of the fast at the end of the month of Ramadan; and Eid al-Adha, the feast of sacrifice that concludes the pilgrimage to Mecca. On Eid al-Fitr, the lesser of these two festivals, Muslims pray, visit friends and family, and exchange gifts. On Eid al-Adha, they sacrifice a lamb or some other animal to commemorate both Abraham's willingness to offer his son Ishmael to Allah and Allah's mercy in accepting a lamb instead. In February 1996 President Bill Clinton welcomed Muslim families to the White House to celebrate Eid al-Fitr, prompting First Lady Hillary Clinton to call that holiday an "American event." In September 2001, the U.S. Postal Service issued a postage stamp (its first on a Muslim theme) celebrating both Eids. The calligraphy on the stamp read "Eid mubarak"—a traditional holiday greeting meaning "May your festival be blessed."

Fatwa: Islamic legal opinion given by a legal scholar (*mufti*) in the context of a particular school of law and in response to a specific question posed by a court or individual. Although many non-Muslims believe that fatwas are infallible declarations, most Muslims understand them to be binding only on those who recognize the authority of the legal scholar who issues them. This term burst into public prominence in the West after Iran's Ayatollah

Khomeini (d. 1989) issued a fatwa calling for the assassination of Salman Rushdie, whose novel *The Satanic Verses* (1988) he deemed blasphemous. More recently, Americans have had to grapple with the 1998 *fatwa* of Osama bin Laden, which stated, "The ruling to kill the Americans and their allies—civilians and military—is an individual duty for every Muslim." Less well known is the July 2005 fatwa issued by the eighteen-member Fiqh Council of North America, which declared, "All acts of terrorism targeting civilians are *haram* (forbidden) in Islam." Many Muslim leaders have observed that bin Laden, who is not a legal scholar, has no authority to issue a fatwa. Even Taliban leader Mullah Mohammed Omar admitted that any so-called fatwas issued by bin Laden are "illegal and null and void."

The Five Pillars of Islam: The key practices of Islam, obligatory for all Muslims. They are: the *Shahadah*, or professing that "there is no god but God, and Muhammad is the messenger of God"; *salat*, or prayer in the direction of Mecca five times a day (dawn, noon, afternoon, sunset, and evening); *satum*, or fasting (from sunrise to sunset) during the lunar month of Ramadan; *zakat*, or almsgiving to the poor (via an asset tax); *hajj*, or pilgrimage to Mecca, once in a lifetime for all who are physically and financially able. Some critics of Islam wrongly claim that jihad is one of the Five Pillars. It is not. Muslims' emphasis on these five pillars underscores the fact that Islam is more focused on right practice (orthopraxy) than on right belief (orthodoxy).

Hadith: Islamic sacred tradition, second in importance only to the Qur'an, relating the words and deeds of Muhammad and his companions as transmitted by trusted confidantes. Muslims interpret the Qur'an in light of these hadith and use their teachings, which they believe to be divinely inspired, to conform their lives to the exemplary life of Muhammad. A given hadith contains two parts: a text and a chain of authority. The latter, which traces the transmitters of the text back to its source, is used to determine how much trust to place in a given hadith (which Muslim scholars classify as *sound*, *good*, or *weak*). Those who have compared the Qur'an in Islam to Jesus in Christianity—for both are the revelations of God—see the hadith as analogous to the Christian New Testament. In any case, it stands alongside the Qur'an itself as one of two key sources of Islamic law. There are six major Sunni compilations, the most authoritative of which are the *sahih* ("authentic") compilations of Bukhari and Muslim (each named after its compiler). Shiites have their own collections of hadith, which include in addition to the sayings and deeds of Muhammad those of their imams.

Hijab: This Arabic term refers to any partition separating two things, but most commonly to a veil or head covering worn by some Muslim women. The Qur'an mandates modesty in female dress but does not say what form this modesty should take. So hijabs vary considerably from country to country and believer to believer, and many Muslim women wear no head covering at all. Since the 1970s the veil has become a battleground between Muslims and Westerners. Many feminists see the veil as the symbol par excellence of the oppression of women in Islam. But many Muslim women, both in the United States and abroad, see head scarves as symbols of Muslim identity and of resistance to the sexual libertinism of Western societies. In the early twenty-first century American courts adjudicated many contests over whether the First Amendment's free exercise clause offers Muslim women the right to cover their hair when doing so would violate dress codes in public schools, jails, police units, or the armed forces.

Imam: To Sunni Muslims, an imam ("leader") is simply the man who leads a congregation in prayer. To Shiite Muslims, an imam is far more important: a descendant of Muhammad chosen by God to lead the community in all areas of belief and practice. Shiites disagree on whether there were five, seven, or twelve imams, but most believe that a *hidden imam* will come in the last days to restore peace and justice on earth. During the Iranian Revolution of 1979 the Ayatollah Khomeini was referred to as an imam, in keeping with the Shiite practice of referring to jurists by that title. In the United States, imam has evolved into a title of respect, akin to Reverend, as in Imam Siraj Wahhaj of Brooklyn, who in 1991 became the first Muslim to offer a prayer before the U.S. House of Representatives.

Islam: The faith of 1.6 billion people and the world's second largest religion after Christianity. *Islam* literally means "submission." Muslims exhibit their submission to Allah (God) by practicing the Five Pillars of Islam: testifying to the oneness of Allah and the prophethood of their founder, Muhammad (ca. 570–632); praying; fasting during the month of Ramadan; almsgiving; and going on pilgrimage to Mecca. Their holy book, the Qur'an, speaks of caring for the poor, a day of judgment, and the bodily resurrection. Their holiest cities are Mecca, Medina, and Jerusalem (in that order). The religion is divided into two major branches: Sunni (87–90 percent of adherents) and Shia (10–13 percent).

Islamism: Also known as *political Islam*, Islamism refers to ultraconservative Islamic movements that use their religion to advance a political agenda. This term is typically pejorative, used as an epithet by critics of such movements as al-Qaeda and Wahhabism. It should not be confused with the term *Islamicist*, which is used in academic circles to refer to scholars specializing in Islam. Seizing on the popularity of the term *Islamist*, some critics of the Religious Right began in the early twenty-first century to refer to politically active conservative Christians as "Christianists."

Jerusalem: Known by Muslims as al-Quds ("The Holy") and mentioned more than six hundred times in the Hebrew Bible, Jerusalem is a sacred place for Jews, Christians, and Muslims and a magnet for both pilgrimage and tourism. As much an idea as a reality, it is built on the metaphors of exile and return and on the blood of the Jewish, Christian, and Muslim martyrs who fought to control it during the Crusades of the Middle Ages. Jerusalem's many holy places include, for Jews, the remains of the Western Wall of the Second Temple, and for Christians, the *Via Dolorosa*, along which Jesus walked to his crucifixion, and the Church of the Holy Sepulchre, on the site where according to tradition he was buried and resurrected. Muslims consider Jerusalem sacred because the angel Gabriel took Muhammad there on his famed "night journey"—from the mosque in Mecca to the Dome of the Rock in Jerusalem, and then to the heavens to converse with prior prophets and to learn how to pray.

Jihad: The term *jihad* is derived from an Arabic word that means "to struggle" or "to make an effort." So to participate in a jihad is to struggle on behalf of God. Muslims distinguish between two types of jihads. The greater is the spiritual struggle of each believer against his or her lesser nature. The lesser is the physical struggle against enemies of Islam, a category that has traditionally included polytheists but not Jews or Christians (whom Muslims classically regard as fellow "People of the Book"). In any physical struggle Muslims are enjoined to fight in accordance with strict regulations (including prohibitions against harming women, children, the old, the sick, and other noncombatants). Those who participate in such a jihad are called Mujahideen, a term popularized by opponents of the Soviet occupation of

Afghanistan. Individuals who die in this sort of battle may be revered as martyrs who go straight to paradise without having to wait (as others must) for the final judgment. Recently, some radical Muslims have tried to modify the strict rules governing the *jihad of the sword*, particularly rules against injuring or killing women, children, civilians, and fellow Muslims. Others have tried to expand the Five Pillars to include a sixth: jihad. Still others have tried to break down the long-standing tradition between holy wars in defense of Islam, which have been widely accepted as legitimate, and offensive holy wars, which have been seen as more dubious. Few Muslims, however, have accepted these reinterpretations. The only groups that stress jihad as holy war are Muslim extremists and extreme critics of Islam.

Martyr: In Judaism, Christianity, and Islam, a martyr (from the Greek word *martus*, "witness") is someone who dies, typically young and violently, for a sacred cause. According to popular Islam, the Muslim martyr, or *shahid* ("witness"), is transported immediately to paradise rather than having to wait for the last judgment. Martyrdom is particularly emphasized among Shiites, whose identity has been profoundly shaped by the suffering and death of Muhammad's grandson Husayn ibn Ali (ca. 626–80) during a battle at Karbala on the banks of the Euphrates in 680, an event commemorated annually by Shiites in the festival of Muharram. During the late twentieth and early twenty-first centuries, martyrdom became a terrorist strategy for suicide bombers in Israel, Iraq, and other countries.

Mecca: The holiest city in the Islamic world, located in modern-day Saudi Arabia. Mecca is holy to Muslims because Muhammad was born there, because he received his earliest revelations in a cave outside the city, and because upon his triumphant return to Mecca in 630 CE he replaced polytheistic worship around the city's Kaaba shrine with monotheistic worship of the one true God. Muslims face Mecca when they pray, and mosques include a niche in the wall (*mihrab*) to orient them in that direction. Going at least once on the hajj, or pilgrimage, to Mecca is a sacred obligation for all Muslims who are physically and financially able. To keep Mecca pure, non-Muslims are not allowed in the city.

Medina: After Mecca Islam's holiest city, Medina, which lies today in Saudi Arabia, is the place where Muhammad fled after leaving Mecca in 622 CE, where he founded the Islamic community (*ummah*), and where he established himself as not only a prophet but also a patriarch, politician, and military leader. It is also the city where he built the first mosque, where he died, and where he is buried. Muhammad's flight in 622 from Mecca to Medina—known as the *hijra*—is such a significant event in Islam that Muslims date their lunar calendar from that moment. (Much of 2007 CE falls for them in 1427 AH—"in the year of the hijra.") During the 1990s, some American Muslims began speaking of transforming the United States into a Medina, by which they meant it was time to establish an American ummah—an Islamic community that was both authentically American and authentically Islamic.

Mosque: The place where Muslims assemble for congregational prayer on Fridays is called a mosque in English or a *masjid* ("place of prostration") in Arabic. Classically, mosques have a minaret from which a call to prayer is issued five times a day. They also feature fountains equipped with running water for ritual ablutions, a niche in the wall facing Mecca called a mihrab, and, near the mihrab, an elevated pulpit from which a sermon is given during Friday worship. Mosques also function as educational centers, where students come for instruction in the Qur'an, hadith, and Islamic law. The three most important mosques in the Muslim world are in Mecca, Medina, and Jerusalem.

Muhammad (ca. 570–632 CE): The founder and last prophet of Islam, and the vehicle through whom God revealed the Qur'an. Muhammad was born in Mecca circa 570 CE, raised as an orphan, and buried in Medina in 632. He received his first revelation from God at roughly the age of forty, when the angel Gabriel appeared to him in a cave outside Mecca and commanded him to "recite." The words he subsequently recited were memorized by his followers and eventually written down as the Qur'an. As a trader, Muhammad was exposed both to indigenous polytheistic traditions and to monotheistic Christians and Jews. The revelations he received emphasized the oneness of God (tawhid). So did his subsequent preaching, which earned him not only his first followers (including his first wife, Khadijah) but also opponents in polytheistic Mecca. Hostility to his preaching there prompted Muhammad to flee with his followers to Medina, where they established the Muslim community (ummah). This flight (hijra) from Mecca happened in 622, which now serves as the first year in the Muslim lunar calendar. In 630 Muhammad and his army conquered Mecca and cleansed the area around the ancient Kaaba shrine of idol worshipers. He died two years later, in 632.

Qur'an (lit. "recitation")**:** The holy book of Islam, the final revelation of Allah, and the ultimate authority for Muslims in law, religion, and ethics. Muslims affirm that this scripture was miraculously revealed by Allah via the angel Gabriel to Muhammad, recited by Muhammad, memorized by his companions, written down by scribes, and later compiled into a codex. The first revelation came circa 610 CE, and the official version was canonized (in Arabic) decades after Muhammad's death in 632. While Muslims affirm that the Hebrew and Christian Bibles were revealed by God, they believe that both scriptures have been corrupted over time. The Qur'an, by contrast, exists today just as it was originally delivered. It is authoritative only in the Arabic original; translations are understood to be human products. It is important to note that, while difficult to create a perfect analogy, the best approach to an analogous understanding (that is, how one feature of Islam relates to a key feature of Christianity) might look like this: Allah = YHWH; Qur'an = Jesus (perfect revelation); Muhammad = Paul; Hadith = New Testament.

Ramadan: Period of obligatory fasting from dawn to sunset, observed by Muslims during the ninth month of the Islamic year. This month, which ends with Eid-al-Fitr, the feast of the breaking of the fast, commemorates the first revelation of the Qur'an to Muhammad. A significant minority of NBA basketball players are observant Muslims, and the decisions of Hakeem Olajuwon, Mahmoud Adul Rauf, Shareef Abdur-Rahim, and others to fast during Ramadan have called public attention to the holiday, just as Sandy Koufax's decision, as a Jew, not to pitch in a 1965 World Series game on Yom Kippur focused public attention on the Day of Atonement. It is now traditional for U.S. presidents to send greetings to Muslims and to host fast-breaking dinners at the White House during Ramadan. Travelers, the sick, the elderly, children, and pregnant and nursing women are generally exempt from fasting during Ramadan.

Shari'ah: This term refers in Arabic to a path to water worn by camels. So shariah is the Islamic path—the body of divinely inspired laws for individual and social life rooted in the Qur'an and the hadith. Muslims distinguish between shariah and fiqh. The former term refers to divine law proper. The latter refers to jurisprudence, or human efforts to interpret that law, and is much more open to debate. Different Shiite groups recognize different schools of legal interpretation. Sunnis recognize five: Hanafi, Maliki, Shafii, Zahiri, and Hanbali. The Hanbali school, which currently predominates in Saudi Arabia and the wider Arabian Peninsula, is often described as the most conservative since it favors literal interpretation of the Qur'an.

Shiite Islam: Along with Sunni Islam, one of the two main divisions in the Muslim tradition, and the smaller of the two. After the death of Muhammad in 632, the Muslim community split over the question of succession. One party, which became the Sunni majority, determined his successors by election, referring to them as caliphs. Another party insisted that Muhammad's successors be drawn from his family. They followed Muhammad's son-in-law Ali, referring to him as their imam and calling themselves Shiites or Shias (lit. "followers" or "partisans"). Unlike Sunnis, who invest only political authority in their caliphs (leaving spiritual authority in the Muslim community as a whole), Shiites invest both political and spiritual authority in their imams. They view as authoritative not only the Qur'an and the hadith but also the teachings of their imams, whom they see as intercessors between themselves and Allah. Shiites disagree on how many imams followed Ali, but the largest Shiite faction affirms a line of twelve and believes that the final imam, who went into hiding, will return at the end of time to restore peace and justice on earth. One key moment in Shiite history was the murder at Karbala in 680 of Husayn ibn Ali, Muhammad's grandson and the third Shiite imam. This event, remembered every year by Shiites during the festival of Muharram, has made Shiites more receptive to the tradition of martyrdom than their Sunni counterparts. Shiism is the most popular form of Islam in Iran and Iraq, and there are large Shiite populations in Pakistan, Indiana, Azerbaijan, Lebanon, Syria, and Afghanistan. Roughly 10 to 13 percent of the world's Muslims are Shiites.

Sunni Islam: Along with Shiite Islam, one of two main divisions in the Muslim tradition, and the larger of the two. Sunnis get their name from *sunna* ("tradition"), which refers to the religious and ethical model set by Muhammad. Sunni Muslims, therefore, are those who adhere strictly to the traditions of the Qur'an and the exemplary sayings and actions of Muhammad—*the way of the prophet*—as recorded in the hadith. Sunnis split from Shiites after Muhammad's death, when Sunnis said that the prophet's successor should be elected by the ummah, or Muslim community, rather than coming (as Shiites insisted) from Muhammad's bloodline. Sunnis invest less authority in their leaders than do Shiites. They view Shiite prayers uttered in the name of Ali or Husayn or other imams as violations of the principle of divine oneness (tawhid). Roughly 87 to 90 percent of the world's Muslims are Sunnis. Countries where Sunni Islam predominates include Afghanistan, Algeria, Egypt, Indonesia, Pakistan, Saudi Arabia, and Turkey.

Taliban: Islamic militants, many of them students (*talib* means "seeker" or "student" in Arabic), who were trained in madrasahs (Islamic schools) in Pakistani refugee camps during the Russian-Afghan war led by Mullah Mohammed Omar (b. 1959). The Taliban began taking control of parts of Afghanistan in November 1994; in 1997, when the Taliban was recognized by several countries in the region as the legitimate government, it governed Afghanistan as a theocratic state with rigid gender segregation, severe restrictions on female schooling, strict punishments (stoning for adultery and amputations for theft), and bans on television, music, and sports. In 2001 the Taliban destroyed two giant Buddhas carved in the third century CE into the cliffs in Afghanistan's Bamiyan Valley. Because the Taliban had provided shelter to Osama bin Laden and his al-Qaeda network, they were attacked and defeated by American and other forces after 9/11. During the Taliban's short reign, only three of the world's fifty-three Muslim-majority countries officially recognized their government.

Tawhid: Arabic for the oneness and uniqueness of God. Expressed in the first half of the Muslim creed the Shabadah—"There is no god but God"— tawhid is the central teaching of Islam and of the Qur'an. This doctrine of radical monotheism denies not only atheism and polytheism but also the Christian Trinity, which Muslims condemn as shirk, or ascribing partners to God. Tawhid has been used throughout Islamic history as a call for unity among the world's Muslims. It has been particularly stressed by Wahhabis, who denounce popular devotions to saints as violations of tawhid.

Wahhabism: Ultraconservative or radical Sunni Muslim revitalization movement that aims to reverse the moral decline of the Muslim world by returning to the pure Islam of the Qur'an and Muhammad. Opponents gave Wahhabis their name, which derives from founder Muhammad ibn

Abd al-Wahhab (1703–92), a scholar of the Sunnis' conservative Hanbali school. But Wahhabis often refer to themselves either as *Muwahhidun* (upholders of divine unity) or as *Salafis*, a broader but closely related school that denounces as apostates Muslims who deviate from the beliefs and practices of the first three generations of Muslims (the righteous predecessors: *Salaf*). Wahhabism, which has been compared with both Unitarianism and Puritanism, rejects as corruptions of the pure faith virtually all medieval and modern accretions to Islam, including popular devotions to saints and Sufi mysticism. Wahhabis are particularly zealous about strict adherence to shariah, or Islamic law. They reject the separation of church and state, and they regard Muslims who do not accept their views as heretics. This movement, which dates to the 1740s in Arabia, won the support of the Bedouin chief Muhammad ibn Saud in 1747 and became dominant in modern-day Saudi Arabia (though many Wahhabis criticized the House of Saud when it opened the nation to Western influences after the discovery of oil in the 1930s). In recent decades Wahhabism spread to Afghanistan under the Taliban regime and, thanks to an aggressive mosque-building program funded by Saudis, into mosques in Europe and the United States. Osama bin Laden and al-Qaeda are both influenced by Wahhabism, but the greater influence on each seems to be the thought of the Egyptian radical Sayyid Qutb.

Zionism: Movement to create a Jewish nation in the land of Zion, namely Israel/Palestine. This movement, rooted in the Jewish hope for a messiah who would fulfill God's promise of a land for Abraham's descendants, dates to the destruction of the First Temple in 586 BCE and the subsequent scattering of the Jews into the diaspora. It took political form in 1897 when Theodor Herzl convened in Basel, Switzerland, the First Zionist Congress, which aimed to create "for the Jewish people a home in Palestine secured by public law." Zionism was initially opposed on the right by Orthodox Jews, who thought that this task belonged to God alone, and on the left by Reform Jews, who did not want to be accused of having mixed loyalties to their homelands. Following the Holocaust, however, a new consensus emerged among Jews and non-Jews alike for a Jewish state, which became a reality in 1948. Today some Christian Zionists support the State of Israel because of their (suspect) belief that the New Testament book of Revelation describes a Jewish state as a prerequisite for the Second Coming of Jesus.

Appendix II

The following is an example of how you, the church leader/pastor/change agent, might engage a difficult subject in a blog format. This is one of the most read blog posts I've ever written. It created much discussion on Twitter, Facebook, and my blog (www.joshuagraves.com). Of course, the point is not to create drama, but to use e-formats for real dialogue.

NYC Mosque Drama
(Park 51 and the Kingdom of God)

As a Christian minister, I am a public leader. Like it or not, it comes with the territory. I know the following will resonate with some and disturb others. I write the following after much study, reflection, and prayer. I write also knowing that a blog is a tenuous place to talk about the things that really matter.

This week I've been reading the *The Good Soldiers*, by Pulitzer Prize winner David Finkel, and paying attention to the debate raging across the media landscape regarding the mosque that could potentially be built near the sight of the Twin Towers (Ground Zero). *Good Soldiers* is a painful account of how absolutely dark war can be, the complexity of nation-state and religion in bed with each other, the perspectives of the soldier (often ignored by both parties in the U.S.) and the sheer difficulty of measuring what is "good" and "redemptive" in a wartime era. The book also masterfully depicts the complexity of the collision between *America's* Christianity and *Iraq's* Islam (not to mention the fact that there are Muslims in the U.S. and Christians in Iraq).

I sympathize with those who are opposed to a mosque being built near Ground Zero. It is a *slap in the face,* in this perspective, to put one of the major symbols of Islam (a mosque or, more appropriately, *masjid—mosque* is the French translation of the Arabic) in the shadow of the deadliest attack from an outside group on American soil. Over three thousand people, innocent people, lost their lives. It was a day of sheer evil and horror. A day that has forever changed the narrative of good and evil in America.

I understand that many U.S. citizens are afraid of Islam, or detest Islam because of certain actions taken by a small minority (it's a religion of 1.6 billion people—the second largest religion in the world behind Christianity, which has just over 2 billion adherents). But the fear/rage is also the result of the lack of leadership on behalf of other Islamic leaders speaking out against the terrorist expression of jihad. The world needs more Islamic leaders to step to center stage and speak out against the insidious violence we see almost every week—just as we needed Christian leaders to speak out against the genocide of Native Americans, the atomic bombs dropped in Japan, the Holocaust in Europe, the murder of eight hundred thousand people in Rwanda, the slaughter in Sudan . . . the list goes on and on. Side note: The majority of Muslims in the world do not live in the Middle East. The majority live outside—for instance, I believe Indonesia has more Muslims than any other single country.

When I asked a Muslim leader at the Al-Farooq Mosque in Atlanta why more Muslim leaders don't speak out, he apologized, agreed, and also noted that "Christians have gone silent during some of the great injustices of human history." Whether one believes Jesus to be the true revelation of God (which I do), his point is well taken.

Perhaps there are a few more things to consider on this public matter. First, I'm appalled at the inconsistency of some in their reading of the First Amendment (many don't know what the First Amendment actually says). That is, conservatives become *intent of the law* (e.g., "The Founding Fathers meant Christianity when they wrote *religion*") interpreters and liberals become strict constructionists (i.e., "It says 'freedom of religion'"). We are all selective interpreters and selective fundamentalists. Until we begin to admit this, we can't cover the ground needed to move forward. We tend to be *selective* when it's in our best interest or fits our particular belief system.

Second, the actual location is two blocks from Ground Zero. Manhattan is a big place. If I understand the facts accurately, there's another mosque even closer that's been there for several decades.

Third, since the Immigration Act of 1965 the ethnic, and therefore religious, landscape of America will never be the same. America can choose to eliminate all Muslims from our society (isolate and imprison), or seek to build authentic relationships for understanding and mutual transformation. What other options are there? I choose the latter because I think the future depends upon it.

Fusing the world of Jesus with the contemporary is a remarkably difficult task. It takes wisdom, discernment, and historical perspective. I personally would not want to treat a minority group in a way that, if the roles were reversed, would silence my religious beliefs. If the leaders of Iran were to ask me if they should allow a church to be built, I would enthusiastically hope for this happen. You may object, saying, "That will never happen in Iran." Perhaps, but if we believe it should, perhaps our duty in America is to show that such mutual respect and mutual commitment for one's deepest convictions should compel all of us to exemplify the best of our traditions, not the worst.

May God grant us the courage to change the things we can, the humility to accept the things we cannot change, and the wisdom to know the difference.

Appendix III

Stereotype Survey Results

Survey #1, September 2011

Note: For questions 5 and 8: M = Muslim, B = Buddhist, J = Jew, Ba = Baha'i, H = Hindu, A = Atheist. All answers are presented exactly as they were given.[1]

1. **When you hear the word *Muslim,* what do you think of?**

   Crazy/Mohammad

   Another religion

   Extremist/religion

   Pakistan

   Monotheistic religion

   Mideast

   Cult

   Religion/radical

---

   1 Special thanks to Audrey Pinson for helping me compile and make sense of this data.

Friends I had that went to Islam school after regular school

A national religion

Middle East

Crusades

Middle East and seventh-grade social studies class

1 billion people

9/11 controversy

Holy war

Mosques and Middle Eastern clothes

Religion/revolt/terrorism

Lost/radical/9.11

Head wraps

Anti-freedom/anti-women

Different religion

Works based middle eastern religion

Mosque with sound of call for prayer

Submission

Strange religion

"the others"

Extremist

Middle East

Backwards—still in the fifth century/inflexible

Submit

Abraham

Mosque

Alien

False

Terror

Muslim

Krismirsaioni—a person

A national religion

2. When you hear the word *Islam*, what do you think of?

Crazy/Mohammad

Terrorist

Research physician's lab tech, lab tech's family (Somalian)

Osama

Person of Islamic religion

Head covering

Extremist

Suspicion

Extremist

I think of them praying on their knees

Convicted people

My brother-in-law (he's Muslim)

Morgan Freeman in *Robin Hood: Prince of Thieves*

Follower of Mohammad

Abuse of women

Mixed

Prayer—devotion

Someone who follows Islam

Mohammed/Allah/Mosque

Thailand worship

Anti-freedom/anti-women

I don't have any one thing, women in head coverings

Adherent of Islam

Male with Middle Eastern look, has facial hair

Friend

Mistreatment/terrorists

Five times per day prayer

Slumdog Millionaire

Koran

Dome of the Rock—call to worship in the Casbah

Pillars of faith

Veil

My friend, Faraz

Practicing alien

Mis-lead

Terror

Palestinian

Follower of teachings of Mohammad

Muslim is white, positive

3. **When you hear the word *Jew,* what do you think of?**

Crucified Jesus

History

Israel/NY delicatessen

Jesus

Follower of Torah

Old Testament

Religious *better than*

Friends

Israel

Wailing Wall

Northeast and Israel

The Final Solution

WWII

Israel

Kosher/Israel

God's chosen people

Old Testament/synagogue

Old Testament

Genocide/Jesus/Lost/Misguided

Jesus was a Jew

Our faith ancestors

I've known Jewish people all my life—I think of friends

Remnants of ancient religion

Man wearing prayer shawl

Israel

Commerce/social consciousness

Conservative evangelical politics and Zionism

Yamakas (sp?)

Traditional

Intelligence

People of the Book

Jesus

The first chosen generation

Holocaust

Chosen

Don't believe Jesus is the Messiah

God's chosen people

Walking streets of NY

4. **When you are in a room with a person of a different religion, are you uncomfortable?**

27 No

Depends

Depends if I'm in the minority in the room

Depends

Only if they're dressed differently

Not typically

Not normally

Not really

No—excited

No, but intrigued

No—unless it is a Muslim

No, except on an airplane; then yes

Sometimes but not always

Sometimes

5. **How many Muslim friends do you have? (Buddhist? Jewish? Hindu?)**

5 None

Very few

Not many

Not many

Not sure, work with/have hundreds of clients who are primarily Sikhs?

Several—I work at a clinic and see so many different religions

A few, not many, lots of Jewish atheists

Limited numbers, some Jewish friends

20

15–20

About 20

J–1, A–4

M–2, J–20, A–1

J–20, A–20

J–6, H–3, A–1

M–2,

A–1

M–2, J–2, A–2

J–2 to 3

M–2 or 3, J–20, A–3

J–2 or 3, A–2 or 3

B–3 or 4, J–70, Ba–2, H–5, A–7 or 8

M–5 or 6, B–1 or 2, J–lots, H–1 to 2, A–10

M–5 to 10, B–1, J–2, Ba–1, H–1, A–1

M–50 to 100, B–5 to 10, J–2, H–2, A–2

M–20 to 30, B–4 to 5, J–10 to 15, Ba–6 or 7, H–30, A–15 to 20

M–1, B–many, J–2, Ba–0, H–0, A–1

M–1, J–10, A–don't know

M–2, J–1, Ba–1, A–lots

M–6, B–2, J–2, A–many

M–1, H–9, several of the others

M–several, J–2 well, Ba–a few, H–a few, A–a lot

J–a few, A–a few

M–1 or 2, J–a couple, A–a couple

M–5 or so, B–less than 5, J–many

J–6, A–too many to count

M–more than 10, B–not sure, J–more than 10, A–about 4

6. Do you ever discuss spiritual matters?

18 Yes

Yes, at times to a Jew, often now

Yes, with a Jew and atheist

Yes, but not with "strangers"

N/A

N/A

No

No

No

No—not often or at all

No (every once in a while)

Not really

Not often but their more colleges than intimate friends

I assume you mean from people in #5 (no) except with my brother who claims to be an atheist

Sometimes

Sometimes

Sometimes, not in work environment

Rarely

Seldom

Occasionally, but not much

Used to—not now

7. If Jesus were alive today, what would he look like?

I picture the drawing of the front of the book: *Christianity: The First Three Thousand Years*

Dark complexion, dark hair

Dark skin, dark hair

Olive complexion, dark hair, medium build, beard

Dark skin, unclean, thin

Possible dark skin—would dress like the rest of us

Like a normal guy

5'10" 165 lbs., nondescript, normal man

Indistinguishable in a metropolis

Not sure. Could be any ethnicity

Undetermined race

Jew

A Jew

A Jew

A Jew

Jewish

Jewish

Dark hair (Jewish)

Probably brown and Jewish

Jewish not sure about the beard

A Muslim

Middle eastern

Middle Eastern ethnicity

Mid-eastern—black string hair, dark complexion, short

Middle Easterner

Like he is from the Middle East

Just a guess, dark complexion—more Middle Eastern

In the same context 2000 years he would look like a middle eastern

Sadam Hussein's oldest son

Osama Bin Laden

Maybe like one of the Indians that work for me?

Odds are, probably Asian

Not a white man w/ a beard

Not really sure . . . maybe the stereotypical fair skin, dark long hair, beard, blue eyes

Dust covered, kind eyes, gentle movements, thin

Slender, medium height, not very light-skinned, light facial hair, soft-spoken but not a passive personality

A plumber

Like me

Not like me

Never think about it

8. **How many Muslims do you think live in the U.S.? Buddhists? Jews?**

One million

4.5 million

300,000

1,000,000

M–3 mil, B–1.5 mil, J–1 mil

M–3 mil, B–10 mil, J–100 mil

M–10 mil, B–5 mil, J–50 mil

M–5 mil, B–10 mil, J–25 mil

M–10 mil, B–5 mil, J–30 mil

M–15 mil, B–2 mil, J–25 mil

B–10 mil, J–20 mil

M–10 mil, B–5 mil, J–30 mil

M–5 mil,B–1 mil, J–20 mil

M–5 mil, B–2 mil, J–6 mil

M–2 mil, B–500k,J–5 mil

M–20 mil, B–5 mil, J–7 mil

M–5 mil, B–500k, J–3 mil

M–6 mil, B–1 mil, J–12 mil

M–15 mil, B–5 mil, J–30 mil

M–5 to 15 mil, B–?, J–a lot

M–75 to 100 mil, B–50 mil, J–75 to 100 mil

M–over 10 mil, B–over 5 mil, J–over 5 mil

M–few million, B–one mil, J–several million

M–5 percent, B–.01 percent, J–6 percent

M–30 percent American population, B–2 percent, J–10 percent

M–1/3 of population, B–thousands, J–1/3 of population

M–a lot, B–not as many, J–a lot

M–a lot, B–few, J–middling

No clue

No clue

No idea

A lot

I would say quite a few

More than Buddhist

A few million Muslim, Jews less Buddhists

Several million Muslims, probably more than Buddhists, fewer
than Jews

9. **Do you see any parallels between being black in the U.S. in
the 1960s and being Muslim today?**

Yes

Yes

Yes

Yes, believe they are victims

Yes, but not to the same extent

Yes, some but lots of differences. More different

Yes—definite discrimination though not as public, my family definitely

Yes—minority, so many people suffering due to a few people's bad
decisions.

Yes, but with no education gap today sensitive attitude toward women

Yes, unnecessary attacks based on skin color

Yes, both viewed as volatile, loners, trouble causing, and against the
norm

Yes—scared of group of people; no—some misunderstanding of Muslims, now is cultural and not religious but blamed on religion

Yes, in terms of being isolated and targeted by people needing enemies
and scapegoats. I'd also say those parallels led many blacks to the
Muslim faith in the '60s and beyond.

Yes—most people fear them/don't understand

Yes—not anyone with a turban is a terrorist similar to blacks being dirty/unclean/unworthy

Yes, from the point of stereotyping. However, African Americans faced more blatant racism.

Sure, due to 9/11 and Bin Laden most Americans assume all Muslims are "evil" and have a fear of them. Some are even going to the extent of prohibiting the building of mosques b/c they believe they are teaching people how to be terrorists.

Exactly

Absolutely and being Japanese during WWII and Germans after WWI

No

No

No

No, we shared a common faith w/ blacks in 60s

No, have not seen Muslim discrimination personally

Not many

Not much

Not really, the discrimination against Muslims is not governmental, it's more subtle

Not really. Currently reading *What Good Is God*; based on this, I don't feel Muslims are nearly as oppressed.

Haven't really thought about it but not really

Yes & no—they are stereotyped. Black is an identifiable skin color, Muslims are multiethnic

Yes and no, Blacks were judged just for color of skin, Muslims are feared.

Yes and no—'60s fear was from something blacks did not do, today fear of Muslims was brought on from what was done to the USA.

?

Some

Some but not the same

Some, better parallel is with "Illegal Aliens"/Hispanic

Some, there is a latent suspicion of Muslims today that probably resembles suspicion of blacks in the 60s. Not only suspicion, but also "insecurity" about the relationships, white versus black

Both seen as "different," both pre-judged

10. Did you ever notice Muslims before 9/11?

21 Yes

Yes, but not as much

Yes—I lived near Dearborn, MI

Yes, they drive a lot of taxis in NYC

Yes, but confused them with sihk and Hindu

Yes, worked with them for years

Yes, I had work with some was in Lebanon in '83

Yes, one of my dear high school friends is Muslim

Patronized a bakery owned by a Muslim

No

No

No

Not often

Not much

Not really

Not really

Not really. I was pretty sheltered

Didn't know any

11. Then/Now: Reactions to 9/11

Fear/sadness—change in the world

Anger, fear, sadness/pride sadness

Sadness/numbness

Anger, frustration/apathy

Anger, hatred, vengeance/understanding of the role of empire in terrorism and the similarities w/ U.S. military action

Sadness, anger, disappointment

Sadness

Horror, panic/hate

Somber

Sadness/still sadness

Anger, disgust, concerned about how people would respond

Did not impact my view of Muslims . . . immediately, sorrow, fear, hate, love/sadness

Sadness, anger, the feeling that the U.S. did not have a clue as to the larger picture of what creates terrorists and hatred against the U.S.

Anger, sadness, fear/same

Anger

Sadness, worry; on 9/12 I took my son to the local Syrian bakery figuring they were going to need the business

Horror, sadness/the birth of my last daughter 2 years after let us reclaim the day but still feel for the families who lost loved ones and a country that no longer feels safe

Hatred, violence back, patriotic, why?/still patriotic, frustration, why?, anger, feelings of senselessness

Sad, mad

Fear, loss/grateful for 10 years of relative safety, angry that Bloomberg is omitting prayer from 9/11 memorial

Fear, sad, horror

Anger, fear/less so now

Fear/lingering ache

Terror, fear, confusion

Sadness, frustration, some anger/wariness, along w/ empathy for the discrimination they experience

Awe that someone or some group could cause so much pain, anger, sadness/I'm a lot more accepting of other cultures now that I've had time to think about everything

Shock, disbelief/I'm more disconnected from it, almost like it never happened since I've never been to NYC or known anyone it affected drastically

Extreme sadness/anger

Sorrow

Sad scared/sad over the bitterness people have, personally I believe it was the result of extremists. Christian extremists do/have done awful things too. Most people are good—the exceptions are bad, not the majority

To me it was a sad and terrible thing, but I did not relate my feelings to a race of people. Two things that relate to my feelings: 1) book, *The Irresistible Revolution*; 2) movie, *My Name Is Khan*. It was a movie about a family who endured suffering after 9/11.

Shock, fear/sadness

Anger/busy

Anger/not as much

Having lived in NY!!! Know people who lived in sight of WTC

Some people are bad

Anger, outrage/sadness, disappointment

Rage, disappointment, disbelief, anger, sadness, pride (in EMS/ Police)/same

Survey #2, December 2011

Note: For questions 5 and 8: M = Muslim, B = Buddhist, J = Jew, Ba = Baha'i, H = Hindu, A = Atheist. All answers are presented exactly how they were given.

1. **When you hear the word *Islam*, what is the first thing that comes to mind?**

Devoted

Muslim

Unified control

Follower of Muhammad, living in the past

World religion, common roots to Judeo-Christian

A rapidly growing faith group

Religion

9/11/01

Religion, head scarfs, Middle East

Middle East

Religion—mainly Middle Eastern—but spreading quickly

East Muslim

Religion of Mid-East, now more powerful than before

Muhammad

Extremely focused/devoted beliefs and culture

2. **When you hear the word *Muslim*, what is the first thing that comes to mind?**

New understanding

God-loving and devotion to Koran

Religion

Call to prayer, near east

Same, but the cultural aspect

Middle East

Middle East

Mosque

Mosques

Very spiritually minded

A follower of Islam

Devout, worship, prayer

Believer in God

Kathryn's former lab tech; religion of Mid-East

Ancient religion—similar to Christianity

Christians that march to a different drum

3. **When you hear the word *Jew*, what is the first thing that comes to mind?**

Jesus

A people that do not believe Jesus is Son of God

God's first choice

Disciplined, smart

Spiritual ancestors, often more cultural than religious

Jesus

God's people

Old Testament

New York

Moses

Old Testament—Moses—still waiting for Messiah

Some of my Jewish acquaintances

God's chosen

Cheap—people of tradition

No belief in Jesus

Closed way of life and religion

4. **When you sit next to a person of a different ethnicity in a public place (restaurant, airplane, movie theater), do you feel uncomfortable?**

Only in certain areas of town. It has less to do with their ethnicity and more to do with location.

No

No

No—attended a rock concert with a Pakistani and her daughters last year

No

No

No

No

No

Not uncomfortable, but maybe more curious than with someone who looks like me

No

No

No—mostly feel observant

No

No

5. **How many Muslims do you know? Buddhists? Jews? Baha'is? Hindus? Atheists?**

M–2; B–4; 2-J; 2–B; 9–H; 3–A

M–20

M–3; B–3; 4–J; 1–B; 2–H; 2–A

B–a few (each daughter has a Baha'i friend)

M–5–10; J–5; H–2

J–4; H–3; A–1

J–several; A–1

M–5; J–10; A–10+

M–unsure; J–unsure

Know several Jews

Lots of atheists; quite a few Jews; a handful of Muslims

B–2; J–10; B–4; A–2

M–10+; A–a few

Many Jews, but less than 5 of others

J–25; A–1

6. Do you ever discuss spiritual matters?

With people in my close community? Nonstop . . . The groups listed above? Not close enough to them.

Not really

No, unless they've become my friends

Yes

Yes, with the Baha'i, seeking understanding

Yes

No

No

Yes

Yes

Not really

Not often, these are more work collegues than social acquaintances

Yes

Yes —mostly superficial

No

Yes

7. If Jesus were alive today, what would he look physically like?

TSA's poster child suspect

A symbol of strength and compassion

Dark complexion/stocky, maybe short build/brown eyes/million-dollar smile

Dark complexion, short, long stringy hair

Not like us Christians—olive skin, beard; interesting to see paintings of Dutch masters at the Frist—they depicted Jesus as having blond hair and blue eyes.

Middle Eastern looks

Should be any nationality

Relatively short; dark hair

Israeli

Someone from the Middle East

It would depend on where he was born—if Bethlehem, he would look Middle Eastern—maybe Indian

Dark complexion; more likely to stand out in a white church than on a metropolitan city street.

Jewish

Regular guy—not high fashion, ordinary, but you would notice him—Words, not looks

Jewish

Tall, slender, male, clean shaven, short hair

8. **How many Muslims do you think live in the U.S.? Buddhists? Jews?**

M–5 million

M–5 million; B–1 million; J–20 million

No idea

M–10 million

M–1,000,000; B–500,000; J–10,000,000

M–1m; B–5m; J–4m

M–3m

J–8m

A lot more than used to I think for all 3

M–2m worldwide

A few million Muslims; more Jews, fewer Buddhists

J–1.2m

M–2m; B–300k; J–50m

M–4m; B–500,000; J–30,000,000

M–7m; B–3m; J–10m

9. **Do you see any parallels between being black in the U.S. in the 1960s and being Muslim today?**

Yes—common thread being fear on both sides for both instances

Some; however, I think Americans have been much quicker to soften their view of Muslims, where it took longer with civil rights.

Some, of course, but Muslims have it easier because of those years.

No

Possibly, but we hadn't been attacked by blacks and weren't at war with several of their countries.

Yes, in that both are judged based on stereotypes. No, in that Muslims generally come to U.S. voluntarily, not on slave ships.

Not in Nashville. Maybe in other areas.

No

Similarities, yes

Yes, racial profiling especially in airports; people unhappy when mosques are being built

Parallels from a racial distrust perspective

Yes

Yes, but different

Yes, prejudice against a race

Not really

Yes

10. **Did you ever notice Muslims before 9/11?**

Not really . . . I just lived in a area of the country that's not diverse at all

Yes

Not really

Yes

Yes— awareness really started with the Iran hostage crises

Yes—my brother-in-law is Muslim non-preaching, however.

Yes

No

Only Middle Easterners

Yes, one of my dear high school friends was Muslim

Women more than men because of their form of dress

Didn't give them much thought, though had some good conversations w/ them in college

Yes

Not really because of being scattered

Resentment/fear/anger

Yes

11. **What emotions did you experience on 9/11?
Ten years later?**

Sadness for the loss of life, but not a full understanding of what it meant or how life/this world was forever changed / Sadness for the loss of life, but now that I'm older, have a deeper understanding for what happened, and can see the effects; I'm also saddened by our response.

Sadness/confused; a small sect misguided

Horror/some fear of future/know it was people "under control" doing what they believed.

Resentment/anger

Fear; anger; seeking wisdom from God—national repentance/sadness, divided as a nation—anger at the political correctness of allowing no clergy at the 9/11 memorial service.

Sadness for all the lives that were lost unnecessarily.

Sadness and anger

Disbelief, anger and sorrow

Sadness, uncertainty

Saddened that someone would think flying a plane into a building is something God would want to happen / Still saddened but happy that event brought our nation together and also sparked interest in learning more about Muslims and their beliefs.

Shock, sadness and some fear/ten years: sad for the country's distrust, and flying which I do regularly is a hassle.

Shock, then ten years later, I'm a lot more likely to eat Middle Eastern food.

Sorrow, crazy time

Fear and anger / apathy

Resentment, fear, anger / still resentment and lack of understanding

Sorror, hate, justice / helplessness and frustration

Bibliography

Bailey, Kenneth E. *Poet and Peasant: A Literary-Cultural Approach to the Parables in Luke.* Grand Rapids: Eerdmans, 1983.

Barton, John. "The Missional Posture and Our Muslim Neighbors." *Missio Dei* 2 (2011). http://missiodeijournal.com/article.php?issue=md-2-2&author=md-2-2-barton.

Bediako, Kwame. *Jesus and the Gospel in Africa: History and Experience.* Maryknoll, NY: Orbis, 2004.

Bell, Rob. *Sex God: Exploring the Endless Connections between Sexuality and Spirituality.* Grand Rapids: Zondervan, 2007.

Branch, Taylor. *At Canaan's Edge: America in the King Years, 1965–1968.* New York: Simon & Schuster, 2006.

———. *Parting the Waters: America in the King Years, 1954–1963.* New York: Simon & Schuster, 1988.

———. *Pillar of Fire: America in the King Years, 1963–65.* New York: Simon & Schuster, 1998.

Camp, Lee. *Mere Discipleship: Radical Christianity in a Rebellious World.* Grand Rapids: Brazos, 2003.

———. *Who Is My Enemy? Questions American Christians Must Face about Islam—and Themselves.* Grand Rapids: Brazos, 2011.

Campbell, Charles L. "The Folly of the Sermon on the Mount." In *Preaching the Sermon on the Mount: The World It Imagines,* edited by David Fleer and Dave Bland, 59–68. St. Louis: Chalice, 2007.

———. *Preaching Jesus: New Directions for Homiletics in Hans Frei's Postliberal Theology.* 1997. Reprint, Eugene, OR: Wipf & Stock, 2005.

Coakley, Sarah. *God, Sexuality, and the Self: An Essay on The Trinity.* Cambridge: Cambridge University Press, 2013.

Council on American-Islamic Relations. *American Muslims: A Journalist's Guide to Understanding Islam and Muslims.* Washington, DC: CAIR, 2007.

Craddock, Fred. *The Collected Sermons of Fred Craddock*. Louisville: Westminster John Knox, 2011.

Curtis, Edward E. *Muslims in America: A Short History*. Religion in American Life. Oxford: Oxford University Press, 2009.

Deane, Claudia, and Darryl Fears. "Negative Perception of Islam Increasing." *Washington Post*, March 9, 2006. http://www.washingtonpost.com/wp-dyn/content/article/2006/03/08/AR2006030802221.html.

Ferguson, Everett. *Backgrounds of Early Christianity*. Grand Rapids: Eerdmans, 2003.

Finkel, David. *The Good Soldiers*. New York: Sarah Crichton, 2009.

Giridharadas, Anand. *The True American: Murder and Mercy in Texas*. New York: Norton, 2014.

Graves, Joshua. *The Feast: How to Serve Jesus in a Famished World*. Abilene, TX: Leafwood, 2009.

Green, Joel B. *The Gospel of Luke*. The New International Commentary on the New Testament. Grand Rapids: Eerdmans, 1997.

Green, Joel B., et al., eds. *Dictionary of Jesus and the Gospels: An Introduction*. Downers Grove, IL: InterVarsity, 1993.

Grossman, Cathy Lynn. "Numbers of U.S. Muslims to Double." *USA Today*, January 27, 2011. http://usatoday30.usatoday.com/news/religion/2011-01-27-1Amuslim27_ST_N.htm.

Hagner, Donald A. *Matthew 1–13*. Word Biblical Commentary 33A. Dallas: Word, 1993.

Hammer, Juliane, and Omid Safi, eds. *The Cambridge Companion to American Islam*. Cambridge Companions to Religion. New York: Cambridge University Press, 2013.

Hays, Richard B. *The Moral Vision of the New Testament: Community, Cross, New Creation; a Contemporary Introduction to New Testament Ethics*. San Francisco: HarperSanFrancisco, 1996.

Jamison, Christopher. *Finding Sanctuary: Monastic Steps for Everyday Life*. London: Weidenfeld & Nicholson, 2006.

Johnson, Luke Timothy. *The Gospel of Luke*. Sacra Pagina. Collegeville, MN: Liturgical, 2006.

Kennedy, John. *A Nation of Immigrants*. New York: Harper Perennial, 2008.

Kistemaker, Simon J. *The Parables: Understanding the Stories Jesus Told*. Grand Rapids: Baker, 1990.

Lamott, Anne. *Bird by Bird: Some Instructions on Writing and Life*. New York: Anchor, 1995.

Levine, Amy-Jill. *The Misunderstood Jew: The Church and the Scandal of the Jewish Jesus*. New York: HarperOne, 2007.

Lewis, C. S. *The Screwtape Letters*. New York: Random House, 1961.

Lippman, Thomas W. *Understanding Islam: An Introduction to the Muslim World*. 3rd rev. ed. New York: Meridian, 1995.

Lischer, Richard. *The End of Words: The Language of Reconciliation in a Culture of Violence*. Lyman Beecher Lectures in Preaching. Grand Rapids: Eerdmans, 2008.

———. *The Preacher King: Martin Luther King, Jr. and the Word that Moved America*. New York: Oxford University Press, 1995.

Manseau, Peter. "The Muslims of Early America." *New York Times*, February 9, 2015. http://www.nytimes.com/2015/02/09/opinion/the-founding-muslims.html?action=click&pgtype=Homepage&region=CColumn&module=MostEmailed&version=Full&src=me&WT.nav=MostEmailed&_r=0.

Bibliography

Mathewes, Charles T. *Understanding Religious Ethics*. Chichester, UK: Wiley-Blackwell, 2010.

McKnight, Scot. *The Blue Parakeet: Rethinking How You Read the Bible*. Grand Rapids: Zondervan, 2008.

O'Connor, Flannery. Selected and edited by Sally and Robert Fitzgerald. *Mystery and Manners: Occasional Prose*. New York: Farrar, Straus & Giroux, 2009.

Patel, Eboo. *Acts of Faith: The Story of an American Muslim, the Struggle for the Soul of a Generation*. Boston: Beacon, 2010.

Peterson, Eugene H. *Christ Plays in Ten Thousand Places: A Conversation in Spiritual Theology*. Grand Rapids: Eerdmans, 1999.

Plantinga, Cornelius, Jr. *Not the Way It's Supposed to Be: A Breviary of Sin*. Grand Rapids: Eerdmans, 1995.

Prothero, Stephen. *God Is Not One: The Eight Rival Religions That Run the World*. San Francisco: HarperSanFrancisco, 2010.

Pummer, Reinhard. *The Samaritans*. Leiden: Brill, 1987.

Reilly, Joanne, et al., eds. *Belsen in History and Memory*. Portland, OR: F. Cass, 1997.

Sayers, Mark. *The Vertical Self: How Biblical Faith Can Help Us Discover Who We Are in an Age of Self-Obsession*. Nashville: Thomas Nelson, 2010.

Seidman, Chris, and Joshua Graves. *Heaven on Earth: Realizing the Good Life Now*. Nashville: Abingdon, 2012.

Smith, Christian, and Melinda Lundquist Denton. *Soul Searching: The Religious and Spiritual Lives of American Teenagers*. New York: Oxford, 2005.

Smith, Jane I. *Islam in America*. 2nd ed. Columbia Contemporary American Religion. New York: Columbia University Press, 2009.

Steimer, Thierry. "The Biology of Fear- and Anxiety-Related Behaviors." *Dialogues in Clinical Neuroscience* 4 (2002) 231–49.

Tate, Curtis. "Obama Honors Citizens 'Who Stopped to Help.'" *McClatchy Newspapers*, October 20, 2011. http://www.mcclatchydc.com/2011/10/20/127880/obama-honors-citizens-who-stopped.html.

Taylor, Barbara Brown. *The Preaching Life*. Cambridge, MA: Cowley, 1993.

Tippett, Krista. *Speaking of Faith: Why Religion Matters and How to Talk About It*. New York: Penguin, 2007.

Untener, Ken. *The Practical Prophet: Pastoral Writings*. New York: Paulist, 2007.

Volf, Miroslav. *Allah: A Christian Response*. New York: HarperOne, 2011.

———. *Exclusion and Embrace: A Theological Exploration of Identity, Otherness, and Reconciliation*. Nashville: Abingdon, 1996.

Warner, Rob. *21st Century Church*. London: Hodder & Stoughton, 1994.

Washington, James Melvin, ed. *I Have a Dream: Writings and Speeches That Changed the World*. San Francisco: HarperSanFrancisco, 1992.

Whitehead, James D. "The Religious Imagination." *Liturgy* 5 (1985) 54–59.

Winner, Lauren F. *Real Sex: The Naked Truth about Chastity*. Grand Rapids: Brazos, 2006.

"The World's Muslims: Religion, Politics and Society." Report of the Pew Forum on Religion & Public Life, April 30, 2013. http://www.pewforum.org/files/2013/04/worlds-muslims-religion-politics-society-full-report.pdf.

Wright, N. T. *Luke for Everyone*. 2nd ed. Louisville: Westminster John Knox, 2004.

———. *The New Testament and the People of God*. London: SPCK, 1996.

———. *Simply Christian: Why Christianity Makes Sense*. San Francisco: HarperSanFrancisco, 2010.

Bibliography

Wuthnow, Robert. *America and the Challenges of Religious Diversity*. Princeton: Princeton
    University Press, 2005.
Yancey, Philip. *What Good Is God? In Search of a Faith That Matters*. New York: FaithWords,
    2010.
Yoder, John Howard. *The Original Revolution*. Scottdale, PA: Herald, 1971.